Journey in Joy

A Lifestyle of More than Happiness

Daniel W. Thompson
PhD, Lt. Col. (Ret.), BCC

2024

TRILOGY
A WHOLLY OWNED SUBSIDIARY OF TBN
PROFESSIONAL PUBLISHING MEETS POWERFUL PROMOTION

Journey In Joy

Trilogy Christian Publishers

A Wholly Owned Subsidiary of Trinity Broadcasting Network

2442 Michelle Drive, Tustin, CA 92780

Copyright © 2024 by Daniel W. Thompson

Scripture quotations marked CEV are taken from the Contemporary English Version®. Copyright © 1995 American Bible Society. All rights reserved.

Scripture quotations marked ESV are taken from the Holy Bible, English Standard Version® Bible. Copyright © 2001 by Crossway Bibles, a publishing ministry of Good News Publishers. Used by permission. All rights reserved.

Scripture quotations marked ERV are taken from the Easy-to-Read Version® Bible. Copyright © 2006 by Bible League International. Used by permission. All rights reserved.

Scripture quotations marked GNT are taken from the Good News Translation® (Today's English Version, Second Edition). Copyright © 1982 by American Bible Society. All rights reserved.

Scripture quotations marked HCSB are taken from the Holman Christian Standard Bible®. Used by Permission. Copyright ©1999, 2000, 2003, 2009 Holman Bible Publishers. Holman Christian Standard Bible®, Holman CSB®, and HCSB® are federally registered trademarks of Holman Bible Publishers.

Scripture quotations marked MSG are taken from *THE MESSAGE*. Copyright © 1993, 2002, 2018 by Eugene H. Peterson. Used by permission of NavPress. All rights reserved. Represented by Tyndale House Publishers, Inc.

Scripture quotations marked MNT are taken from the Montgomery New Testament® Bible. Copyright © 1861, 1924, and 1934 by The American Baptist Publication Society. Used by permission. All rights reserved.

Scripture quotations marked NASB are taken from the New American Standard Bible®. Copyright © 1960, 1962, 1963, 1968, 1971, 1972, 1973, 1975, 1977, 1995 by The Lockman Foundation. Used by permission. www.Lockman.org.

Scripture quotations marked NET are taken from the New English Translation® Bible. Copyright © 1996-2017 by Biblical Studies Press. Used by permission. All rights reserved.

Scripture quotations marked NIV are taken from the Holy Bible, New International Version®. Copyright © 1973, 1978, 1984, 2011 by Biblica, Inc.™ Used by permission of Zondervan. All rights reserved worldwide.

Scripture quotations marked NKJV are taken from the New King James Version®. Copyright © 1982 by Thomas Nelson. Used by permission. All rights reserved.

Scripture quotations marked NLT are taken from the Holy Bible, New Living Translation. Copyright © 1996, 2004, 2015 by Tyndale House Foundation. Used by permission of Tyndale House Publishers, Inc., Carol Stream, Illinois 60188. All rights reserved.

Scripture quotations marked NRSV are taken from the New Revised Standard Version® Bible. Copyright © 2021 by National Council of the Churches of Christ in the United States of America. Used by permission. All rights reserved.

Scripture quotations marked RSV are taken from the Revised Standard Version® Bible. Copyright © 1946, 1952, and 1971 by National Council of the Churches of Christ in the United States of America. Used by permission. All rights reserved.

Scripture quotations marked KJV are taken from the King James Version of the Bible. Public domain.

All rights reserved, including the right to reproduce this book or portions thereof in any form whatsoever.

For information, address Trilogy Christian Publishing

Rights Department, 2442 Michelle Drive, Tustin, CA 92780.

Trilogy Christian Publishing/TBN and colophon are trademarks of Trinity Broadcasting Network.

For information about special discounts for bulk purchases, please contact Trilogy Christian Publishing.

Trilogy Disclaimer: The views and content expressed in this book are those of the author and may not necessarily reflect the views and doctrine of Trilogy Christian Publishing or the Trinity Broadcasting Network.

10 9 8 7 6 5 4 3 2 1

Library of Congress Cataloging-in-Publication Data is available.

ISBN 979-8-89041-981-1

ISBN 979-8-89041-982-8 (ebook)

To Those on Their Own Paths, Pursuing Joy

Acknowledgments

So many people were helpful to me in the writing process of *Journey in Joy*. My late mother, who continually exuded joy throughout her 19 years of battling cancer, inspired me to take a serious inward look into my attitudes and then a deep dive into the topic of joy. Without her seed planted within me, I may have never considered listening to the Holy Spirit's nudge to learn more about joy.

During several years of reading written prayers and devotionals I posted on social media, Donna Sanchez needled me to write an inspirational book. Her belief in me gave me reason to believe in myself. Once I took that first step in writing this publication, my wife Erica not only became an optimistic cheerleader and ongoing sounding board for ideas, but she demonstrated the patience of a saint when I spent uninterrupted hours reflecting, studying, and typing. Pat Morris and Chaplain Jenna Carson also offered frequent encouragement, keeping a fire underneath me to persevere in my writing and finish strong. Three trusted friends, Rev. Rob MacReynolds, Katie McCarthy, and Veronica Tovar, believed in this project so much that their contributions enabled me to begin the publishing process.

When I needed him most, pastor and theologian Preston Cravey took time out of his busy schedule to read through difficult sections, validating and verifying for biblical accuracy. A dear Christian friend and spectacular writer, Anne Furman, read my initial drafts and laboriously edited every page, leaving invaluable suggestions and corrections where needed. Nancy Bosarge, a former newspaper journalist, served as my second editor. She graciously exercised her talents to review, recommend, and revise my work, no matter how arduous the drafts became.

I should also thank my esteemed daughter Abigail for her eagerness to compose the Forward to this book. In her own right, she has published a couple of Christian fantasy fiction novels, all while in her teens! Her passion for writing helped pave the way for me to learn how to do the same. Whenever I felt like quitting, I would glance over to her desk and see her scribbling down new ideas and developing plots or subplots for her future series. That alone motivated me to endure.

Finally, I want to say that every page of this devotional was written with someone in mind. It is the person for whom life needs direction for pursuing and choosing joy. If you are that wounded person to whom I am speaking, I pray that the Lord will use my efforts to strengthen you with the Truths of Scripture and repair your shattered faith. Creating a lifestyle of joy will not be easy, but in the end, it will transform not only your spiritual health but also your physical well-being.

Table of Contents

Acknowledgments 7
Table of Contents 9
Foreword 11
Preface 13
Introduction 15

Day 1	Joy in God's Presence	25
Day 2	Joy in God's Creation	29
Day 3	Joy in God's Word	33
Day 4	Joy in God's Law	37
Day 5	Joy in God's Approval	41
Day 6	Joy in God's Presence	45
Day 7	Joy in God's Provision	49
Day 8	Joy in God's Greatness	53
Day 9	Joy in Hope	57
Day 10	Joy in Faith	61
Day 11	Joy in Trust	65
Day 12	Joy in Repentance	69
Day 13	Joy in Faithfulness	73
Day 14	Joy in Obedience	77
Day 15	Joy in Salvation	81
Day 16	Joy in Assurance	85
Day 17	Joy in Gratitude	89
Day 18	Joy in Humility	93
Day 19	Joy in Contentment	97
Day 20	Joy in Forgiveness	101
Day 21	Joy in Love	105
Day 22	Joy in Service	109
Day 23	Joy in Giving	113
Day 24	Joy in Peacemaking	117

Day 25	Joy in Fruit	121
Day 26	Joy in Prayer	125
Day 27	Joy in Advising	129
Day 28	Joy in Soul-Winning	133
Day 29	Joy in Praise	137
Day 30	Joy in Singing	141
Day 31	Joy in Fellowship	145
Day 32	Joy in Celebrating	149
Day 33	Joy in Labor	153
Day 34	Joy in Suffering	157
Day 35	Joy in Tears	161
Day 36	Joy in Weakness	165
Day 37	Joy in Poverty	169
Day 38	Joy in Discipline	173
Day 39	Joy in Persecution	177
Day 40	Joy in Perpetuity	181

Index	187
References.	189
About the Author	196

Foreword

When I first heard that my Daddy was writing *Journey in Joy*, I leaped for joy because this world needs more joy. It is obsessed with fear. Everything around us whispers of our addiction to fear. Whether we are conscious of it or not, our society loves the soul-sucking, adrenaline-inducing emotion of fear. Turn on the news, click on your phone or laptop, pick up a book, and each one will tell you that this world is decaying rapidly. Now, I'm not here to tell you that the world is not distressed. I am not here to argue that the world feels heavy, ripe with the rottenness of pain. I'm here to remind you that hopelessness has not won.

We can have hope because *"perfect love casts out fear"* (1 John 4:18 NKJV). We can have hope because the perfect love of God allowed His son to die on the cross so that we could be forgiven and have an assurance of where we will be able to spend eternity. We can have hope because of Christ's victory over death. Without hope, however, there can be no joy. One cannot have joy if one has no hope; that would be like asking a lamp to burn without oil, rain to fall without water, and the sun to shine without gas… impossible. Hope comes before joy like a seed planted in what becomes a growing, sprawling tree pulled heavy with fruit. There must be hope at the center of joy because joy is possible when we rest in something Greater than what we can see.

Joy is the evidence of hope, peace, love, and all the other fruits of the Spirit pulling the limbs down with their weight of harvest. These fruits help us feel the joy that bursts from our breasts, which in a world like ours can feel elusive and shadowy without substance.

Paul and Silas demonstrated evidence of hope, peace, and love when they sang in prison with joy, not because they were foolish or naïve. I am sure their bruises and lash marks stripped them of the naivete of the cruel world. Instead, it reminded them of the ever-creeping beast known as satan, who prowls seeking his prey. So why did they sing? Yes, the answer is joy, but the answer is also hope. They couldn't have had joy in that moment if they did not have hope in a God bigger than the lashes on their backs and the cement cells around their bodies. They hoped for a brighter day that did not rest in mercurial nations and kings but instead for a Promised Land on the other side of their last breath. They hoped in a God who they knew would bring justice to the world, even if the cruelty of it felt suffocating at times.

Journey in Joy is much like a roadmap on how to find the type of joy Paul and Silas experienced while incarcerated in a dungy prison. Beware, however, the prince of this world or the things of this world may try to rob you of your joy, especially when you find hope in anything but God. Trying to find hope in yourself, others, the media, a sports team, or anything else will bring darkness. Instead, having hope in the Lord can only brighten your pathway because He is the light who dispels the darkness (1 John 1:5).

If you find that this devotional guide has blessed you with not just as sense of hope, but of flourishing joy, I encourage you to share it with others who can also experience the brilliant light of joy that will chase away their darkness of fear and uncertainty.

Abigail Grace Thompson

Preface

"**L**ieutenant Colonel Thompson," the Air Force First Sergeant choked on his words, "I have a Red Cross message for you." No deployed service member ever wants to hear such a message because invariably, it is associated with tragic news. As an Air Force Chaplain, I had delivered many Red Cross messages and witnessed the grief that followed such an emergency alert memo.

My fear when joining the military was not that I might die for my country but that I might receive a Red Cross message while deployed because that would usually mean someone whom I loved may have died or may be close to death. Sadly, my greatest fears were realized while I was sequestered in the heart of the war-torn country of Afghanistan in 2020. By God's grace, I was able to catch multiple flights across the globe to finally sojourn with my mother, who was suffering from a terminal cancer that rapidly metastasized. Just before she was no longer able to speak, Mom shared her final words with me, "Danny, I love you. Thank you for traveling around the world to see me. My body may be weak and frail, but joy comes in the morning."

Since my mother's passing, I have long deliberated on her final words. What is joy, and what did she mean by "joy comes in the morning?" Could I ever experience her level of sheer joyful contentment as she graduated from this temporal world? These questions and others inspired me to pursue a journey of how to find pure, authentic joy. What I learned in the trenches of God's Word and a daily walk with Jesus is what I will share over the next forty days.

Introduction

Getting the Most from This Book

I will never forget the journey of driving home to McGuire Air Force Base from visiting Ocean City, New Jersey. It was another steamy July filled with promise and activity. My wife was carrying our second child, and our first son sucked on his pacifier while he sat in the car seat of our second-hand minivan. Life was nicely rolling until I looked down at the newly illuminated fuel gauge light. *Houston, we have a problem,* I privately thought to myself. There were no navigational devices back then. Cell towers were non-existent in rural areas, and my road atlas omitted the symbol that I needed most… a gas station.

As would any concerned husband and father, I began to sweat nervously. I sweat out of fear that we would get stranded on an abandoned-looking country road without any way to call for roadside assistance. Out of an abundance of caution, I decided to optimize our fuel economy by turning off the air conditioner and rolling down the windows. By this time, I was sweating even more, not so much from the 100% humidity, but out of distress for how many lashes I would get from my pregnant wife. By God's grace, we finally found a gas station, and I was spared fifty lashes.

If I learned any lesson that hot summer day, it was not to wait until my meter reads empty. The same is true for our spiritual journey with God. We cannot wait to refuel our souls until our resilient meter reads empty. Like any journey on the road, fill-ups and tune-ups are necessary if we wish to keep moving. Regular maintenance may be vital, but what we feed our tanks is also critical. Choosing a premium grade fuel over the lowest octane fuel diluted with ethanol may not only extend your time driving but preserve your engine. What you choose to fill your heart and soul with may be the difference between an optimal spiritual journey or one that sputters and clogs your engine.

Journey in Joy was written with a premium-grade mindset so that you can optimize your spiritual impact due to the divine truths embedded in each devotional. Though tempting, I encourage you to resist the urge to keep reading into the next day's lesson. *Journey in Joy* is more than a book; it is a roadmap to a forty-day journey in the joy of the Lord that will walk you through adversity, various trials (1 Peter 1:6–7), suffering (Hebrews 12:2), sorrow (2 Corinthians 6:10), and so much more. Each day will explore a different biblical onramp to joy, bringing fresh humor, divine truths, prayer prompts, and practical application.

But why forty days? Forty days is not some magical number pulled out of thin air. In the Bible, the concept of forty often appears in various contexts, and it is associated with themes of testing, preparation, cleansing, and transformation. Perhaps the most well-known instance of the forty-day period is Jesus' forty days of fasting and prayer in the wilderness (Matthew 4:1–11). Dwelling in the arms of the Father gave Him the human strength to persevere.

Earlier in the Old Testament, the number forty is often associated with preparation and renewal. For example, the great flood in the story of Noah lasted for forty days and nights, during which the world was cleansed and renewed. Moses spent forty days on Mount Sinai to receive the Ten Commandments, representing a period of divine revelation and preparation for leading the Israelites. Elijah was fortified when the Lord blessed him with forty days of strength from a single meal.

Do you want more strength? According to Nehemiah 8:10 (NKJV), *"The joy of the Lord is your strength,"* and is brought to completeness when we consent to His portion of righteousness by grace that brings us together so we can delight in His presence. Whether you are going through a time of testing, preparation, cleansing, or transformation, spending quality time with the Lord will lead you to immense joy and strength. By disciplining yourself over the next forty days—guided by Scripture verses and timeless principles—your journey will be set in the right direction to make a lifestyle of lifetime joy.

Disciplining yourself to experience joy involves a willful choice, such as setting aside time to abide with God, giving thanks in all things, meditating on Scripture, or fulfilling your purpose by serving Him. Lifestyle habits like these are much like the process of growing tomatoes from seed to harvest. Without regularly attending the garden, seedlings may never grow.

Tossing tomato seeds onto rocky ground will only make the seeds vulnerable to becoming dried out by the sun or consumed by animals. On the other hand, sowing seeds in a high-quality potting mix often combined with peat, vermiculite, and perlite will set the right conditions for a healthy plant. Moistening the soil, controlling the right amount of light, and providing adequate circulation are all actions that can help inspire a tomato plant to grow.

Time and timing are also quite vital. If a tomato were grown instantly, it would lack the proper nourishment, juicy qualities, and robust flavor you would expect. The interesting fact about horticulture is that no matter how many ways you try to encourage tomato growth, bearing fruit is completely out of your hands. Only God has the power and authority to will a ripe tomato into existence.

The same is true for joy. Only God has the power and authority to ripen joy into your life because spiritual joy is a "Fruit of the Spirit" (Galatians 5:22–23). Manifesting the Fruit of the Spirit does not come naturally; then, how can we live out the fruit of joy? Theologian Dietrich Bonhoeffer explains it best this way, "Fruit is always the miraculous, the created; it is never a result of the willing, but always of growth. The fruit of the Spirit is a gift of God, and only He can produce it.[1]

When the Holy Spirit indwells a believer, the "fruit" becomes the product of the Holy Spirit's cultivation of character in your heart beyond your natural abilities. Scripture emphasizes that your nature is in direct opposition to the Spirit and, thus, you are unable to produce joy or any other fruit without Him (Galatians 5:17). Paul echoes this understanding of joy in 1 Thessalonians 1:6 (ESV) when he explains how Christians *"received the word in much affliction, with the joy of the Holy Spirit."* Later in the Book of Romans, the Apostle Paul reinforces the fact that joy derives not from the natural but spiritual influences, for the Kingdom of God is a matter of *"peace and joy in the Holy Spirit"* (Romans 14:17 ESV).

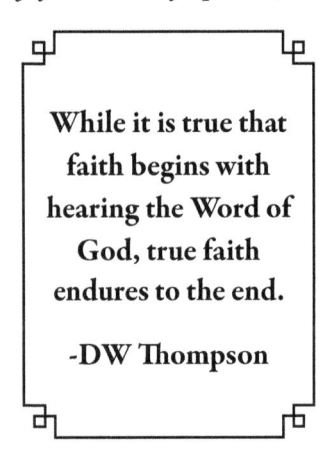

> **While it is true that faith begins with hearing the Word of God, true faith endures to the end.**
>
> -DW Thompson

The joy of the Christian believer is not the fruit of the human spirit in response to satisfying circumstances. Rather, a Christian's joy is a fruit of God's Spirit fulfilled in the believer because of the ultimate sacrifice Jesus made on the cross. While you may not necessarily be able to bear spiritual fruit on your own, if you accept Jesus Christ as your personal Savior, His Spirit will come and live within you. As a result of this gift of salvation, you automatically inherit the fruit of joy.

To manifest this gift of joy that resides in every believer, let us turn no further than John 15:4 (ESV), where Jesus says, *"Abide in me, and I in you. As the branch cannot bear fruit by itself, unless it abides in the vine, neither can you, unless you abide in me."* Simply put, Christians are promised that the fruit of God's Spirit will be produced in you when you remain in Him. Your part is to abide. His part is to provide.

---

1 Dietrich Bonhoeffer and Eric Metaxas, The Cost of Discipleship, First Edition, (New York: Touchstone, 1995).

God will provide joy as believers choose to abide. You get to choose joy when you decide to follow His plan for growing your fruit. What might that plan entail? *Journey in Joy* helps to offer a forty-day strategy to prepare the heart for spiritual joy to sprout. The devotional guide is an almanac for believers who wish to schedule a lifestyle of setting the right conditions for joy to grow.

When you dig roots deep in His Word, you will have the best consistency of nourishment to see fruit come into existence. When you have the Son-light guiding your pathway to growth, fruit will come into existence. When you spend quality time being moistened by the baptism of the Holy Spirit, ripened fruit will come into existence. These pathways to growth are a sure thing because God's promises never fail. However, beware of the false fruit that may pop up, imitating the authentic fruit of God.

Gardeners are often enticed by exotic, attractive plants. Feeding into this lure, several online stores sell seeds for rainbow tomatoes, claiming they will produce diverse, vivid colors of tomatoes from the same fruiting stem. Tomatoes come in different hues of red, red-orange, yellow, green, brown, and so on. However, one tomato stem cannot produce different fruit colors. A Black Russian tomato will only produce reddish-brown fruit, while a Green Zebra tomato will only produce striped-green tomatoes. What these scam establishments sell are fake seeds. Their online images of multi-colored tomatoes are digitally enhanced frauds.

Different kinds of fruit can masquerade as the real thing but fail upon closer inspection. Jesus deals with this mismatch in a stunning episode about a fig tree covered in leaves, fraudulently signaling that it should have early figs (Matthew 21:18–22). The Messiah pointed out that it is one thing to lack fruit out of season; it is yet another thing to lack fruit while pretending you have it.

Spiritual joy might be enhanced by its extra foliage, yet it can be mistaken for natural joy that is manufactured by your nature or the circumstances around you. This form of joy has no supernatural influence of the Holy Spirit to produce it. Jesus illustrates natural joy in His parable of the four soils where the seed was sown on rocky ground,

> *As for what was sown on rocky ground, this is the one who hears the word and immediately receives it with joy, yet he has no root in himself, but endures for a while, and when tribulation or persecution arises on account of the word, immediately he falls away.*
>
> (Matthew 13:20–21 ESV)

In this example from Christ, there is no explicit or implied mention of the person having genuine saving faith or evidence of conversion. While it is true that faith begins with hearing the Word of God (Romans 10:17), true faith endures to the end (Matthew 24:13). To be saved is to be preserved in the faith to the end, kept by the power of God through faith unto salvation (1 Peter 1:6).

The joy represented in this passage does not share the character of the Lord's joy because it vaporizes like the dew when the blazing sun of suffering rises in the horizon. The joy vanishes because it was not a joy in God, nor was it a Fruit of the Spirit that has the supernatural ability to delight in God regardless of the circumstance. Instead, this natural joy imitated the vibrant colors of spiritual joy for a fleeting moment, quickly withering for it was not rooted in the True Vine.

As portrayed in Jesus' parable, non-believers can experience joy on this earth. This revelation may come as a shock to some, but it is because of God's grace. Interestingly, the Greek word for joy is "*chara*," and it is closely related to the Greek word "*charis*," which means grace.[2] Chara is the normal reaction to charis, where joy can be experienced by believers and unbelievers because of God's grace.

The grace referred to here is "common grace." Common grace includes all undeserved blessings that natural man receives from God, such as rain, sun, fortune, strength, happiness, natural abilities, and talents. When speaking to a crowd of unbelievers, Paul and Barnabas preach to the mob about how God has given them *"rain from heaven and crops in their seasons;"* they continue saying that God provides them with *"plenty of food and fills [their] hearts with joy"* (Acts 14:17 NIV).

Do you see what the two Apostles were communicating? They were drawing on the doctrine of common grace and Christ's lesson that God makes His sun rise on both evil and good, and He sends *"rain on the just and on the unjust"* (Matthew 5:45b KJV). Paul and Barnabas were telling the crowd to look at the joy they had in their hearts and evaluate who or what might be behind that joy.

In these biblical examples of natural joy resulting from God's common grace, notice how the excitement and happiness of their experiences swiftly dissipate. While unbelievers can and do experience a portion of natural joy, that form of joy is not enduring. Generally speaking, this is because happiness is merely external, fleeting, and is only attainable on Earth. Happiness is often based on happenings that come and go. These worldly pleasures are like meteors that give a radiant and instant flash, then disappear. However, the joys that Christians have are internally abiding... supernaturally sourced by an eternal, unchanging Lord.

The type of joy referenced throughout your forty-day journey is a spiritual joy, as opposed to a natural or worldly joy. What you will discover is a spiritual joy that is inward, hidden within the heart like a wellspring of water that runs underground. What you will not find

---

2   Barry Ferguson, In Collision Course: How to Harness the Power of Love to Heal Your Broken Life, (New York: Morgan Publishing, 2016).

is a reference to a worldly joy that goes no further than the surface, planted on the rocky soil (2 Corinthians 5:12). That type of natural, worldly joy is based on superficial hope in things, all of which are situational and flimsy. Spiritual joy remains subsurface. While enduring suffering, Christians can encounter spiritual joy that is invisible to the outside world because "Thy Word" is hidden in their hearts, and joyful music whistles in melodies that others cannot hear (Psalm 119:11 KJV).

Within the pages of *Journey to Joy*, you will read about a spiritual joy that is sweeter than all the worldly joys (Song of Solomon 1:1). The sweetness is so sweet that it makes everything else sweet, much like the process of pouring sweet water onto flowers to stimulate a more pronounced fragrance and aroma. Because divine joys are so ineffably delicious, the fake, impure, natural delights become tasteless to the tongue. The worldly joys quickly lose their flavor or become bitter. And yet, in contrast, spiritual joy is pure, like a wax-less honey that never expires. Too much natural joy kills the desire for more. However, you can never get tired of drinking the joys of Heaven; they are never overwhelmed, and you will always be satisfied, never to thirst again (John 4:14).

Throughout your season of reading *Journey in Joy,* and after completing your forty-day devotionals, satan may try his hardest to steal your joy. Red Cross messages and other bad news may arrive knocking on your door, yet this is when the joy of the Lord should blossom most in your soul. The temptation to be grafted into worldly stems may become attractive by their vibrant allure and robust foliage; however, resist the urge because *"weeping may endure for a night, but joy comes in the morning"* (Psalm 30:5b NKJV). The sorrow you face in your journey is temporary, but you can choose joy... a heavenly joy before the pain even begins. It starts now over the next forty days by establishing a lifestyle of sowing seeds of *truth* and reaping the fruit that only the

Lord can grow in your life. Treat it as your Christian duty, your moral obligation, to be joyful. After all, *"the godly are happy; they rejoice before God and overcome with joy"* (Psalm 68:3 NET).

*Begin
Your
Journey
Today*

Day 1

Joy in God's Presence

You make known to me the path of life; in your presence there is fullness of joy;

(Psalm 16:11a ESV)

Two hunters came across bear so big that they dropped their rifles and ran for cover. One man climbed a tree while the other hid in a nearby cave. The bear was in no hurry to eat, so he sat down between the tree and the cave to reflect upon his good fortune. Suddenly, and for no apparent reason, the hunter in the cave came rushing out, almost into the waiting bear, hesitated, and then dashed back in again. The same thing happened a second time. When he emerged for a third time, His companion in the tree frantically called out, "Woody, are you crazy? Stay in the cave till he leaves!" "Can't," panted Woody, "there's another bear in there!"[3]

---

[3] "Dilemian: Two Hunters and a Bear Story," Author Unknown, n.d., Sermon Illustrations, Accessed January 16, 2024, https://www.sermonillustrations.com/a-z/d/dilemma.htm.

Sometimes we find ourselves running from God, right into the presence of something grisly. Much like the game of "hide and seek," we experience the thrill of dashing away while the "seeking" person has his or her eyes closed. One thing is for sure... we can run, but we cannot hide from God's pursuit. Jonah ran, and yet ended up in a big fish where he felt the Lord's presence (Jonah 1:17). Elijah ran, yet ended up in a cave where God's presence comforted him, reminding him that he was not alone (1 Kings 19:18).

God never intended for us to be alone. He allows us to experience the joy of His presence. The Jewish people knew that. The nation of Israel centered gatherings around the presence of God. God's presence led the Jews through the wilderness. His presence won them victories. His presence displayed power in the Holy of Holies. His presence proved that He was with them and for them.

According to David, when we are in the presence of God, *"there is fullness of joy"* (Psalm 16:11 ESV). Why? Because God is the sole source of all joy––He is joy. He made us for joy, and the joy of living life reflects the same joy God enjoyed when He created us. Still, to possess the joy of God, we must first be possessed by the joy of God. That means we must consistently make it a routine to go to the altar of the God of *"exceeding joy"* (Psalm 43:4 ESV). Only when we choose to stop running and bask in His presence will the joy of the Lord become our strength (Nehemiah 8:10).

> **To possess the joy of God, we must first be possessed by the joy of God.**

When we decide to stop scrambling in fear, worry, or doubt by simply abiding in Him, the passage states that God will make known to us *"... the path of life"* (Psalm 16:11 ESV). We will not have to ask for directions to get our *bear*ings. By remaining in His presence, our paths will be made straight (Proverbs 3:6). This does not mean we will not meet danger. It is not a matter of *if* but *when* we will face a grisly situation on our journey, yet God promises He will be there for us (Hebrews 13:5). A roaring temptation may appear too much for us to handle, but God promises a way out of temptation (1 Corinthians 10:13). We do not have to *bear* this world alone. His presence will show His power and win us victories.

There will be times when we cannot *bear* staying in our caves, circle of friends, or comfort zones any longer. When we drop our rifles, we need to run into the arms of our Father. The more we rest in God and keep His presence in our lives, the more we will give off the essence of joy. Regardless, this will take time, spending time being in His presence and making it a lifestyle of patiently waiting for the Lord to move. He is often in no hurry. He expects us to be quiet and listen. After all, being still opens the door to hear God's still, small voice speaking. Likewise, when we hear His loving voice, we will experience the fullness of joy.

Action Challenge: List distractions that hinder you from being in the presence of God (i.e., technology, tasks, gossip, anger). Be creative in removing those barriers to be still before God.

_____

_____

_____

_____

_____

_____

_____

Prayer: Loving Lord, fill me with the joy of Your presence. Let every worry and fear disappear to allow Your joy to take over. Help me to feel near to You always. In Jesus' name, amen.

Joy is a sure sign of the presence of God.

Day 2

Joy in God's Creation

Let God enjoy his creation.

(Psalm 104:31b MSG)

On the sixth day, God created the animals and man. Adam saw that each creature had a mate except for him, so he asked the Lord for a companion to ensure he would not have to walk the journey alone.

> "God replied, "Well, Adam, I can create a mate for you. She will be the crown of my creation, and it will be good, very good. She will take care of you always and give you all the respect that is deserving of you. The only thing is, it will cost you an arm and a leg." Adam thought for a second and wondered what he might get for a rib instead.
>
> When Adam awoke from his deep sleep, he looked up and said, 'Wo... man!'"[4]

---

[4] "Joke: After God Created Adam," Author Unknown, Reddit Post, R/Jokes, 2020, www.reddit.com/r/Jokes/comments/ie86sy/after_god_created_adam_adam_came_to_god_and_said/.

God means for us to be stunned and awed by His good craftsmanship, yet not for its own sake. He desires for us to always look at His *masterpiece* and say: If the work of His hands is so full of splendor and beauty, what must the Father Himself be like? His creation is but the shadow of His glory. What will it be, then, to see God in person and not just His works? The grandeur of a billion galaxies does not satisfy the human soul, only God alone.

When God enjoys His creation, so too does the Son. He was there at Creation. Together, they share an overflowing mutual joy in each other's perfections. Creation is an expression of the overflow of abundant joy the Father and Son have in one another. Since creation points to the Creator who rejoices in His works, why shouldn't His people then rejoice in God's creation (Psalm 104:31)? May we join all of creation in rejoicing before the Lord (Psalm 96:13)! Like God, we find joy in creation because it is a reflection of His goodness. Throughout Genesis 1, the point is made six times that God declares His work to be good. When we see God's work, we are reminded of His goodness... that He is coming back to free the world from sin and suffering. Because of His goodness, no more disappointment, distress, disease, or death will rule the world. Because of His goodness, we can experience joy by drinking in creation's glory.

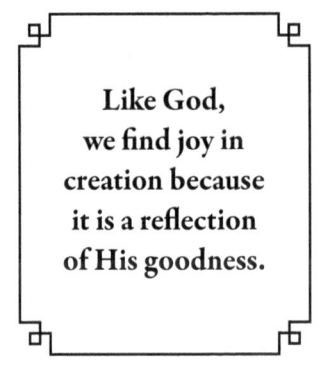

> **Like God, we find joy in creation because it is a reflection of His goodness.**

To find joy in His creation, carefully listen to the sounds in the world around us. Birds chirping in a nest, the wind rushing through mighty trees, or children laughing while playing in the sprinkler. To find joy in His creation, we must feast our eyes on the wonders of the natural world, like a sunset at dawn or a lunar eclipse on a crisp night. When we marvel at celestial glories, we pay Him a compliment by joining in His enjoyment. Make time to view clips of animal bloopers or search for elephants running to rejoice in the birth of a little elephant calf. Creation is all around us. Eat a sweet plumb in early autumn; let its juices explode in the mouth. Pause a moment to feel silk or rub a baby's cheek. To find joy in His creation, we must make a lifestyle of experiencing nature's goodness by intentionally engaging our different senses.

Some say that the real reason Adam and Eve were so joyful was because they had no in-laws. She did not have to hear about his mom's cooking, and he did not have to hear about all the other men she could have married. Humor aside, the real reason they were filled with joy was that they were surrounded by nature throughout their journey. In the coolness of the day, they walked about the Garden enjoying the breeze from God's presence (Genesis 3:8). At night, they looked up and saw the stars blaze. They saw goodness and personal design. Just as God has given us a fingerprint that no one else has, we can leave an imprint that no one else can… an imprint sealed with our joy.

Action Challenge: Take time to savor God's good creation through the five senses--your ears, your eyes, your taste, smell, and touch. Also, take time to savor the work of your hands, what you have accomplished by God's grace. This brings joy!

_____
_____
_____
_____
_____
_____

Prayer: O Father, You have filled the world with beauty. Open our eyes to behold Your gracious hand in all Your works. That we may ... [rejoice] in Your whole creation ... for the sake of Him through whom all things were made, your Son Jesus, our Lord. In Jesus' name, amen.[5]

Joy is our best response to God's creation.

---

5 "Prayers for Joy in God's Creation: Prayers from the Common Book of Prayer," Washington Free Methodist Church, 2024, https://pluto.sitetackle.com/16409/?subpages/Common%20Prayer.shtml.

Day 3

Joy in God's Word

When I discovered your words, I devoured them. They are my joy and my heart's delight...

(Jeremiah 15:16 NLT)

Joe's wife bought a new line of expensive cosmetics guaranteed to make her sparkle and look years younger. After a lengthy sitting of applying the "miracle" products before the mirror, she asked her husband the cringeworthy question as to what age he thought she looked. Examining her carefully, Joe replied, "Judging from your skin, 20; your hair, 18; and your figure, 25."

"Oh, you flatter me, dear!" she gushed.

"Hey, wait a second!" Joe sassed. "I haven't added them up yet."[6]

---

[6] Paster Tim, "Expensive Cosmetics," The Cybersalt Site, January 11, 2023, https://www.cybersalt.org/pearly-gates-jokes/expensive-cosmetics.

Truth without grace is mean. Grace without truth is meaningless. Truth with grace is meaningful. Meaningful truth does not have to hurt; it can bring blessing (Psalm 119:1). In John 17:17 (NIV), Jesus prays to His Father, saying, *"Sanctify them by the truth; your word is truth."* He is conveying two important facts: God's Word equals *truth*, and it is by that Truth that God sets us apart for holy service to Himself. God's Word blesses us, lights our path, and fills us with joy. Psalm 19:8 (NIV) makes that clear, *"The precepts of the Lord are right, giving joy to the heart."*

Joy came to the masses when Ezra read them the Word (Nehemiah 8:10). Joy came to David when he searched the Word as *"one who finds great spoil"* (Psalm 119:162 NIV). Joy came to Jeremiah when he discovered God's words. In fact, he devoured them. They became his *"joy and ... heart's delight"* (Jeremiah 15:16 NLT). Why? Because delighting in God's Word leads us to delight in God, and delighting in God leads to lavish joy. After all, the primary purpose of reading the Bible is not knowing the Bible but knowing God. When we know God, we know the *source* of all joy. No matter what our forefathers ratified, life is not about the pursuit of happiness; it is about joy in the pursuit of God.

Charles Spurgeon echoed this sentiment, "This great joy is sometimes aroused by the fact that there is a Word of God."[7] If God's Word is all we have, we have all we need (John 14:8). The fact that we have the scriptures, wherein God reveals himself, is a great treasure, a "spoil." Unless God had revealed himself, we could never have fully known Him or the richness of His joy.

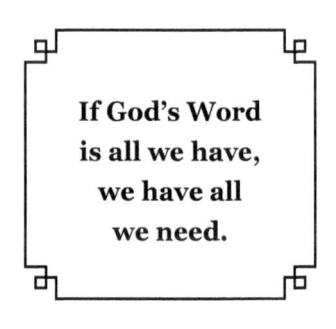

> **If God's Word is all we have, we have all we need.**

---

7   "Great Spoil Sermon by Charles Haddon Spurgeon | January 22, 1882," The Spurgeon Library: The Spurgeon Center and Midwestern Baptist Theological Seminary, 2017, https://www.spurgeon.org/resource-library/sermons/great-spoil/.

When we make it a lifestyle to read God's Word, we find joy in His guidance. How many times do we wonder what we should do or where we should turn, only to open the Word of God and find clarity there? What joy we experience when the mist fades and our path becomes obvious. We can find joy in the freshness of God's Word as well. How often have we come to read a section of Scripture and it comes alive so that it feels like we have never previously read it? The old becomes new; the ancient story comes with fresh power. Uncovering truth from God's Word can bring us as much joy as discovering buried treasure.

Uncovering golden nuggets in God's Word requires a regular routine along our journey. Do not settle for charlatans who flatter us with fool's gold and "miracle" products designed to help shape the figure of our joy. The truth is, when everything is added up, nothing compares to the delight that can be found in the fortune of joy. Despite this joy of God's Word takes constant application. "A Bible that's falling apart usually belongs to someone who isn't."[8]

---

8   "A Quote by Charles Haddon Spurgeon," Goodreads, Inc., 2024, https://www.goodreads.com/quotes/397346-a-bible-that-s-falling-apart-usually-belongs-to-someone-who.

Action Challenge: Avoid reading a meme that talks about God's Word. Go directly to it in search of a jewel. Ask God to show you one specific thing that He wants you to know today. What word does He want you to carry around in your heart?

_____

_____

_____

_____

_____

_____

_____

Prayer: God of truth, I ask that You let my mind meditate on it, let my tongue speak of it, let my heart love it, let my mouth preach it, and let my soul hunger for it so that my joy may be full. I pray this in the One who is the Way, Truth, and Life. In Jesus' name, amen.

Joy sparkles when it's discovered in the rich soil of God's Word.

Day 4

Joy in God's Law

*The precepts of the Lord are right,
giving joy to the heart.*

(Psalm 19:8a NIV)

A dad decided to take his family on vacation when they came across a large sign that read, "Road Closed. Do Not Enter." The man continued around the sign because he was confident it would save them time, despite his wife's better judgment. This road warrior boasted about his gift of discernment until they hit the ten-mile marker and a washed-out bridge. He did a quick U-turn and made his way back to the original warning sign that said on its reverse side, "Welcome back, silly!"[9]

---

[9] Humor | Ministry127, "Joke: Do Not Enter," Author Unknown, Accessed January 28, 2024, https://ministry127.com/resources/illustrations/humor?page=2.

Journeys have no shortcuts to any place worth going. If we take shortcuts, we get cut short. In fact, when it comes to temptations, we all fall short despite the many warning signs and the law (Romans 3:23). When we think of the law, it usually conjures up pictures of judges, police officers, and lists of rules. God's Law is joyfully different. According to David, the statues of the Lord gave him deep joy (Psalm 119:111). Paul declared, *"For in my inner being I delight in God's law"* (Romans 7:22 NIV). Christians can likewise find joy in God's Law.

The moral law of the Lord is a GPS for our journeys. God is the divine mapmaker. He designed the pathways. He knows which way we should head. He sees which road will lead to joy while other actions will end in frustration, emptiness, or destruction. Take, for example, the laws given to the Israelites. They were lightyears ahead of the surrounding nations in terms of health, hygiene, treatment of women and slaves, matters of justice, and so forth. When other nations and leaders became acquainted with the laws of the Heavenly Father, they marveled at God's wisdom and celebrated! The Lord's Law is meant to protect us, not harm us, or keep us from the things we enjoy. The law of the Lord guides us on our journey, helps us, and keeps us in alignment with His will so we might experience the fullness of joy on our path to pursuing holiness (John 15:11).

While joy saturates our hearts when we make it a lifestyle choice to love Jesus and His statutes (Psalm 19:8), we must protect that joy from legalism--substituting extra rules and regulations for our relationship with the Savior. Christ plus works subtly creep into a believer's life by taking the focus off what God has done and placing the focus on what we do for Him. At times, we

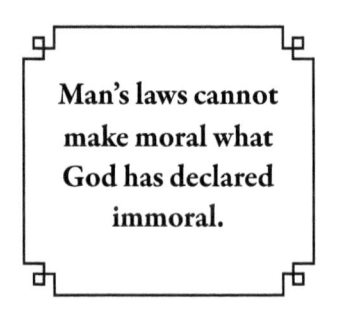

> **Man's laws cannot make moral what God has declared immoral.**

can become so heavenly-minded that we are no earthly good. The Pharisees, for example, expanded the Ten Commandments into 613 other laws. They refused to pluck a hair or dress a wound on the Sabbath because that was considered "work."

Most people agree that good laws promote good and restrain bad in human society. However, because of our broken world, not all human laws are good. "Man's laws cannot make moral what God has declared immoral."[10] God's instructions are good—they are also good for us. They are good because He is good. His laws give comfort in times of anguish, hope in times of despair, wisdom in times of crisis, and joy in times of reflection.

When we decide to go around His road signs, we assume the end will justify the means. Nevertheless, in the end, there are no dead ends in God's plans for us, just a future (Jeremiah 29:11). No matter how silly we feel about going the wrong way, we still have time to U-turn.

---

10   "Quote by Elder Dallin H. Oaks," A-Z Quotes, 2024, https://www.azquotes.com/quote/864259.

Action Challenge: The letter of the law is about you doing everything. The spirit of the law is about God doing everything through you. If you want to embody the spirit of the law, then be intentional this week to allow the Holy Spirit more room to work in and through you. Meditate on Matthew 22:36–40. As you do this, what you will find is that you will be fueled with joy to help you love God and love people better.

_____

_____

_____

_____

_____

_____

_____

Prayer: Jesus, help me to embrace and think rightly about Your law. Thank you for sending the Holy Spirit to help me discern what's right, avoid legalism, and delight in Your precepts. In Jesus' name, amen.

God's Law is no killjoy; it restrains what kills joy.

Day 5

Joy in God's Approval

Go ... drink your wine with a joyful heart, for God has already approved what you do.

(Ecclesiastes 9:7 NIV)

One day, John went to an auction. "While there, he bid on a parrot. He really wanted this bird, so he got caught up in the bidding. "John "kept on bidding but kept getting outbid, so he bid higher and higher and higher. Finally, after he bid way more than he originally intended," John won the bid--the parrot was his at last! As he was paying for the parrot, John wanted assurance from the auctioneer that the parrot could indeed talk before taking it home. "'Don't worry,' said the auctioneer, 'He can talk. Who do you think kept bidding against you?'"[11]

---

[11] "Joke: One Day a Man Went to an Auction," Author Unknown, Reddit Post, R/Jokes, March 20, 2018, https://www.reddit.com/r/Jokes/comments/85s6yg/one_day_a_man_went_to_an_auction_while_there_he/.

Authentic approval cannot be auctioned off, nor can it be earned. A person is not a true friend if we have to tell them "yes" to everything in order to gain favor. All the people we thought were our friends may be the first to turn against us on our journey because as long as we live for man's approval, we will die by man's approval. One true friend whom we can count on is Jesus Christ. He told a story about two men entering the temple looking for God's approval. The first man gave a long prayer, cataloging all he had done. The second man did not do that because he knew his life fell far short of God's expectations. He prayed, *"God, be merciful to me, a sinner"* (Luke 18:13 NKJV). Jesus said the second man went home justified or approved by God.

The approval of God is not earned but received, much like joy is not earned but received. When Paul says, *"We are not trying to please people but God,"* he is not trying to please God to be approved (1 Thessalonians 2:4 NIV). He is trying to please God because he has been approved. Similarly, whether we eat or drink, we can do it with a joyful heart because *"God has already approved"* what we do (Ecclesiastes 9:7 NIV). It does not come to us on a basis of merit but on mercy. A lifestyle of doing right does not flow from an attempt to win the approval of God. It flows from the joy of receiving the approval of God through Jesus Christ our Lord. If we live for the approval of God—if that is the bedrock of our self-worth and identity, we can find comfort and lasting joy.

Those who kneel before God can stand beyond anyone's disapproval. When the Lord is big in our lives, people have less power over us. Their influence is diminished when God is big in our lives. On the flipside, when people become big in our lives, God's joy is diminished because we

> **Those who kneel before God can stand beyond anyone's disapproval.**

are snared by the fear of man (Proverbs 29:25). "If we try to please everyone, we will please no one."[12]

There is nothing wrong with men possessing approval. The wrong comes when approval possesses men. It is important to please our parents, spouses, bosses, and even parrots. Great people make people feel great; little people belittle people. However, we cannot become obsessed with how they might bid against us or think of us on social media. We must remember that it is nice to be important, but it is more important to be nice.

Our goal should not be to gain the applause of man (John 12:34) but the appeal from Heaven. What higher approval could a person enjoy than to know that what he or she has done during this journey of life is pleasing to God? We are to delight in honoring Him. It should be our greatest desire to please our *redeemer* because God's approval is all we need (2 Corinthians 10:18). He will never auction off that approval. Instead, when we believers enter Heaven, we will long to hear, *"Well done, good and faithful servant ... Enter into the joy of your master"* (Matthew 25:21 ESV).

---

12   Goodreads, Inc., "A Quote by Ricky Gervais," 2024, https://www.goodreads.com/quotes/9260914-if-you-try-to-please-everyone-you-ll-please-no-one.

Action Challenge: Identify your boundaries and relationships. Practice saying "yes" to God in the mirror and saying "no" to anything that does not align with your lifestyle goals.

___

Prayer: Lord, it is true that You are the only One whom I need to please. Today, help me not to compromise myself or be a slave to pleasing others. Show me how I can bring You pleasure. In Jesus' name, amen.

While the key to successful joy is pleasing one Lord, the key to failure is pleasing everyone.

Day 6

Joy in God's Presence

I take joy in doing your will, my God, for your instructions are written on my heart.

(Psalm 40:8 NLT)

A passe of men were sitting around the cooler discussing the meaning of life. One turned to ask the others, "If tomorrow all your loved ones found themselves at a funeral gathered around your casket, what would you want to hear them say?" One of them explained how he hoped he would be a good father and husband. Another chimed in how he would like loved ones to express their awe for how he lived the best life with success.

The last guy joked, "I'd want them to say, 'Look, he's moving!'"[13]

---

[13] "Meaning of Life Jokes - 29 Hilarious Meaning of Life Jokes," Upjoke.com, Accessed January 28, 2024, https://upjoke.com/meaning-of-life-jokes.

It is great that we are moving, but it is even greater if we are moving with purpose. You see, the purpose of life is a life of purpose. With the fulfillment of purpose, we inherit a deep and lasting joy. Because each of us on life's journey has a purpose, we should all experience abundant joy (Proverbs 19:21). Everyone wants joy and purpose no matter one's background, age, or situation, yet the pathway to meaningful purpose and joy is found by making a lifestyle of drawing near to God's presence where there is fullness of joy (Psalm 16:11). When we abide in Him, His desires become our desires (Psalm 37:4). His purpose becomes our purpose. When we follow His instructions and do God's will, we will receive joy (Psalm 40:8). There is no greater satisfaction than being right in the center of His perfect and pleasing will (Romans 12:2).

It is His will; it is His purpose that we experience joy. God longs for His joy to become our joy when we follow the biblical map He designed (John 15:11). Scripture shows us that the meaning of life on this earth is far more than simply *living our best life*. The meaning of life is to pursue our gifts, and the purpose of life is to use those gifts. Yes, it can be very difficult to figure out what to do in this life. Ultimately, when we make an effort to tap into our spiritual gifts and talents fearlessly, we will have joy when our journey lands. We will have joy because we get to make a difference in this world by inspiring others and building the Kingdom.

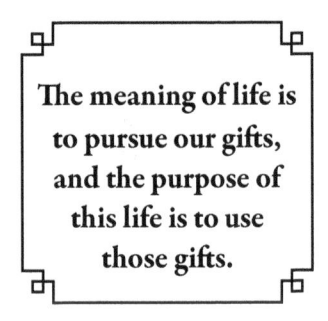

> The meaning of life is to pursue our gifts, and the purpose of this life is to use those gifts.

A person, for instance, who finds tremendous satisfaction and joy in entertaining may have the gift of hospitality. To some, that may seem draining, yet for others, that electrifies their souls. This deep and lasting joy comes from being what the hospitable were created to be, doing what they were called to do (Romans 8:28).

Everyone can experience that same level of joy because everyone has been given gifts and talents that we can use to find our purpose in this life. We are God's masterpiece, designed to do the good things He planned for us long ago (Ephesians 2:10). God created us on purpose, for a purpose. He knit together our abilities in our mother's wombs—for the purpose of His glory (Isaiah 43:7). And so, no life is a mistake or a meaningless consequence of random evolutionary mutations. Every life has a purpose, ripe with joy.

One day, every journey will finally come to an end. We will be held accountable, not by a passe of men sitting around a cooler, but by the Son of Man (John 5:26–29). Did we pursue the gifts He gave us? Did we use them for God's glory? Did we move with purpose? If we did, we may have discovered that the meaning of life is to give life a meaning... a meaning that our purpose is not about us but our Lord. John Piper puts it this way, "He is most glorified in us when we are most satisfied in Him."[14] Now, that should move us with joy.

---

14   John Piper, When I Don't Desire God Publisher: Crossway Books, (Wheaton, Illinois: Crossway, 2004), p. 13.

Action Challenge: Take a spiritual gift survey to reveal what gift(s) God has given you. Match your interests, passions, and gifts with opportunities. Walk with a mentor through this process.

_____
_____
_____
_____
_____
_____
_____
_____

Prayer: Oh God, equip me with abundant joy to fulfill the plan and purpose You have for me to do. Use each gift and talent that You have graciously given to me for Your praise and glory. In Jesus' name, amen.

> *The chief purpose in life is to glorify God;*
> *the chief product is joy.*

Day 7

Joy in God's Provision

...at the works of Your hands I sing for joy.

(Psalm 92:4 ESV)

Every morning, Mary stood on her porch praising God. Day after day, her disgruntled neighbor, Bob, became outraged by her joy. He had enough. When he heard her praising Jesus on her porch while pleading for God to provide some groceries, Bob hatched a plan to humiliate Mary by "proving" there was no God. Bob went to a supermarket, bought a van full of groceries, placed them on her front porch, rang the doorbell, and then hid in the bushes to see what she would do. When Mary opened the door and saw the groceries, she erupted in dance and song before the Lord.

Suddenly, Bob jumped out of the bushes, yelling to Mary how he put the groceries there, not God! Her faith was not shaken. Instead, Mary praised Jehovah-Jireh, "Oh God, You not only provided me groceries, You made the devil pay for them!"[15]

---

15 Paul M. Miller, Compiler, The World's Greatest Collection of Church Jokes: Nearly 500 Hilarious, Good-Natured Jokes and Stories, (Uhrichsville, OH: Barbour Publishing, 2013).

God performs miracles of provision in unlikely ways since His ways are not our ways. He drew water out of a rock during the Israelite's desert journey (Numbers 20:11), produced endless flour and oil for a widow's family (1 Kings 17:14), fed multitudes with five barley loaves and two fish donated by a boy (John 6:9).

Just prior to feeding the crowd of 15,000, Jesus called the disciples to proclaim the gospel and heal the sick (Mark 6:16). He did not call the equipped; He equipped the called. Jesus provided them the authority and power they needed as they went out two by two. When they regrouped, Jesus saw they were hungry and exhausted, so He took them up near Bethsaida to revitalize their anointed journey, again in an unlikely manner.

When the disciples made it up to the rocky hill, a multitude was awaiting them. Naturally, they began to make excuses to send the crowd home (Mark 6:36). Surely, this was not what they had in mind for being refilled by the Lord. Then again, there was something refreshing in the multitude for the disciples. Scripture tells us that while the dinner meal was a gift to the multitude, the multitude was a gift to the disciples. It was the multitude that pulled out the excess of power to feed the crowd supernaturally. Without the multitude, they would not have experienced the full authority of Christ. When the disciples rounded up the five loaves and two fish, they put the portion in Jesus' hands. He raised the food and gave thanks, bringing joy and feast to everyone (1 Thessalonians 3:9).

How often do we find ourselves in impossible circumstances with no human solutions? "Sometimes God lets you hit rock bottom so that you will discover that He is the rock at the

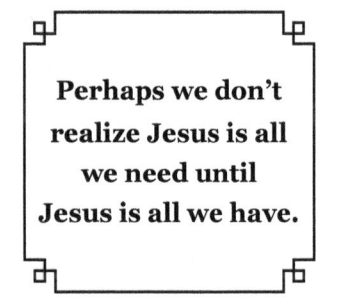

> **Perhaps we don't realize Jesus is all we need until Jesus is all we have.**

bottom."[16] Perhaps we do not realize Jesus is all we need until Jesus is all we have. At the same time, we have not because we ask not (James 4:2). It is when we make it a lifestyle of putting our portion in Jesus' hands that we will finally find miracles of glorious increase (1 Corinthians 3:7). Much like the psalmist who sang for joy at the works of God's hands, we, too, can rejoice because God is always meeting our needs (Psalm 92:4).

Our cup can be complete with joy from a lifestyle of continually praying for God's provision. However, beware of the unexpected distractions that jump out from behind the bush or the foreordained "multitudes" along the journey, divinely designed not to drain but sustain us with access to His wealthy reservoir of power. Let us never forget His power to provide for our fresh water, oil, bread, and groceries, even if the Lord gets the devil to pay for them. Now, that is a glorious reason to rejoice!

---

16   "Quote by Tony Evans," Quotefancy, 2024, https://quotefancy.com/quote/1724205/Tony-Evans-Sometimes-God-lets-you-hit-rock-bottom-so-that-you-will-discover-He-is-the.

Action Challenge: Paying it forward is not a one-time event. Buy a coworker coffee, feed a widow, or bring joy to the lonely. Set a chain reaction, not by paying it back, but by paying it forward one good deed at a time with riches He has provided (Titus 3:14).

_____
_____
_____
_____
_____
_____
_____

Prayer: Dear Lord, thank You for being my daily provider. Help me not to fear times of adversity; rather, help me to trust in You and Your ways more so that I may have joy. In Jesus' name, amen.

God's provision of joy follows His vision for our journey.

Day 8

Joy in God's Greatness

*The LORD has done great things for us,
and we are filled with joy.*

(Psalm 126:3 NIV)

The dictator of a small country was pleased to see his image and likeness observable anywhere in the land. He was really thrilled about the nation's postmaster producing a letter stamp with a picture of his face on it. The dictator relished how great it was to have his effigy in every home in the country as well as every passageway. After the stamp's production, the dictator was greatly displeased that it was not selling very well, so he summoned the chief postmaster to discover why. The postmaster explained how people were complaining that the stamps did not stick. Then, the dictator snatched one from the postmaster, licked it, and stuck it onto an envelope, showing how it sticks flawlessly. "Uh-oh," the postmaster reacted timidly, "I see what's the problem. People have been spitting on the wrong side."[17]

---

17   Bob Phillips, The All-New Clean Joke Book, (Eugene, OR: Harvest House Publishers, 1990), 75.

A great distinction between man and God is that man thinks he is great, but God knows He is great. His Word claims, "Great is the LORD and most worthy of praise; his greatness no one can fathom" (Psalm 145:3 NIV). God's greatness makes Him stronger than all the gods of the universe and all the rulers of the world (Psalm 86:8–10). After all, God without man is God. Man without God is nothing. He is king of all, even of those who deny His power (Hebrews 1:3–4). The greatness of God speaks to His one path to salvation. It speaks to His endless resources and inconceivable power to do as He pleases and for whomever He pleases. His greatness speaks to His creation, which is not about the significance of man but the greatness of God. He made us small and the universe big to tell us something about Himself.

A girl asked the Lord if it was true that a thousand years was like a minute to Him. God agreed. Then she asked the Lord if it was true that a thousand dollars was like a penny to Him. God also agreed. Then, the girl asked the Lord if she could have a penny for her journey. To which the Lord said, "Sure, just a minute."

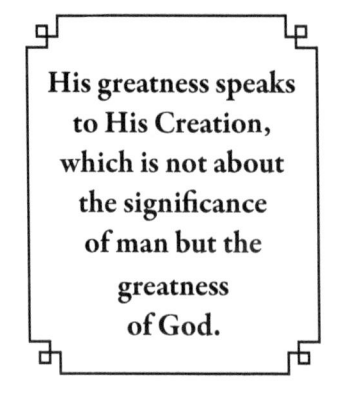

> **His greatness speaks to His Creation, which is not about the significance of man but the greatness of God.**

The measure of God's greatness is incomprehensible. We will never be able to know "too much" about the Lord, for we will never run out of things to learn about Him on our journey to joy, and so we will never become tired of delighting in the discovery of more and more of His excellence and the greatness of His works. Because of His great works, the Psalmist tells us that we will be filled with joy (Psalm 126:3). The Hebrews' author also reminds us that when we make a lifestyle of worship kneeling before our Maker, we come into the heavenly Jerusalem to gather with *"an innumerable company of* [unseen] *angels,"* whose presence should fill us with both awe and joy (Psalm 12:22 NKJV).

Only when the awe of God's greatness rules our hearts will we have joy when people fail us and life stumbles. Awe means our hearts will be filled more with a sense of blessing than a sense of want. We must not allow awe amnesia to become joy anorexia, where the awe of God is replaced with the awe of self. When we do, heartfelt worship dies along with its joy. When we do, that which we spit towards Heaven, we spit on the wrong side since it falls back onto our face. However, if we truly see the greatness of God—the glory of God—His image and likeness will be stamped on our hearts, changing us from one degree of joyful glory to the next (2 Corinthians 3:18). Then and only then, those who kneel before God can stand before anyone who thinks they are God.

Action Challenge: Isolate yourself from all distractions, then lift your hands in praise before God for His greatness through heartfelt worship. Sing along with Hillsong's *The Greatness of Our God* or Michael W. Smith's *Agnus Dei* to ignite your joy.

___

___

___

___

___

___

___

Prayer: Almighty God, we stand in awe of You, who is great and greatly to be praised. No one can fathom Your greatness, for without You, we are nothing. Without You, we cannot; without us, You will not. Thanks for involving us in Your master plan. In Jesus's name, amen.

It's not great joy you need; it is joy in a great God.

Day 9

Joy in Hope

The hope of the righteous is joy...

(Proverbs 10:28 HCSB)

A man out fishing had just anchored his dinghy when another boater came zooming by. The boater happened to be his doctor, who circled back around saying, "Mr. Rich, it is so good to finally see you because I've been wanting to talk with you. I have some bad news and some really bad news for you. Which do you want first?" The old man suggested that he get the bad news first, so the cardiologist continued, "I checked the reports from your exam last week, and things are so serious that you only have one week to live." You may be wondering what could be worse than that, yet the doctor persisted, "The really bad news is, I have been trying to get in touch with you for the last six days!"[18]

---

18   Jack Lord, Now That's Funny: Humorous Illustrations to Soup Up Your Talks, Sermons, or Speeches, (Eugene, OR: Resource Publications, 2017), p. 42.

Rather than catching fish, this man caught bad news. When we get really bad news, what is our first reaction? Hopelessness and despair can settle over our minds like a fog stealing our joy. This was the crushing feeling that Jesus' followers experienced after the crucifixion. Not only were they struck with grief and despair, but they were also struck with questions. The man they had placed their complete hope in was gone. Not just dead... gone. His grave was empty. He had vanished, yet His grave clothes remained.

Experts say you can live weeks without food, days without water, and minutes without oxygen. Despite that, there is no life without hope. Without their hope in Christ, His followers were not *living*, they were just existing. Was their faith in vain (1 Corinthians 15:14)? Absolutely not! Outside of the empty tomb, Jesus revealed Himself as a gardener to a weeping Mary Magdalene. When she recognized His voice as the risen Savior, she rushed to tell the others with exuberant joy.

> **Experts say that you can live weeks without food, days without water, and minutes without oxygen. But truly, there is no life without hope.**

Once Mary's hope was restored, there was instantaneous joy. That is because *"The hope of the righteous brings joy"* (Proverbs 10:28 ESV). Just as we cannot have faith if we do not first have hope, we cannot have joy if we do not first have hope (Hebrews 11:1). When her attention turned from her situation to her *savior*, Mary's hope returned. Hope anchored around things such as jobs, relationships, fame, alcohol, or money is just wishful thinking. Except, certain hope is anchored on the person of Jesus Christ, who never changes, lets you down, or lies (Titus 1:2). *"We have this hope as an anchor for the soul"* (Hebrews 6:19 NIV).

Once Mary realized how Jesus fulfilled His promise to rise again, she rejoiced. Her hope was *"built on nothing less than Jesus' blood and righteousness,"[19]* as the old hymn goes. By conquering death, Christ gave us all hope that His anchor will never let us drift in the everyday currents or storms of life because He holds true to His promises. This includes the promise to forgive all our sins so we can have the hope of eternal salvation and joy.

While on our journey to joy, have we dropped anchor but kept drifting into waters of doubt, fear, or discouragement? We may be known as Mr. or Mrs. Rich, yet we find ourselves poor in spirit because of bad news. We need to cut those lines attached to things or situations and re-anchor in the Lord. No matter what events we encounter, we can experience joy in hope if we are anchored on Christ, the hope of Heaven and the source of true joy.

---

19   "My Hope Is Built on Nothing Less by Edward Mote, 1834," Hymnary.org., Accessed January 15, 2024, https://hymnary.org/text/my_hope_is_built_on_nothing_less.

Action Challenge: Write out at least five promises you can drop anchor to so that you can live a lifestyle without unknowingly drifting into unsafe areas. Consider these promises: God's joy gives strength (Nehemiah 8:10), God advocates for me (John 14:16), God is with me (Joshua 1:19), God is faithful (Hebrews 10:23), God forgives all my sin (1 John 1:9), and God gives abundant hope (Romans 15:13). We must then hold true to our promises to Him.

_____

_____

_____

_____

_____

_____

Prayer: Oh God, I confess how easily I drift. Help me to claim Your promise that You will never allow me to be tempted more than I am able to handle. Anchor me to Jesus when it looks like defeat. May I exhibit a lifestyle of hope in this hopeless world. In Jesus' name, amen.

Without the joy of Jesus: a hopeless end.
With the joy of Jesus: an endless hope.

Day 10

Joy in Faith

> *Though you do not now see him, you believe in him and rejoice with joy that is inexpressible and filled with glory.*
>
> *(1 Peter 1:8b ESV)*

An army recruit was assigned to a paratrooper course. The instructor explained the operation of parachutes. A recruit asked what would happen if the chute didn't open. The instructor answered, "That, Private, is what is known as jumping to a conclusion!"[20]

---

[20] Michael Hodgin, 1002 Humorous Illustrations for Public Speaking: Fresh, Timely, Compelling Illustrations for Preachers, Teachers, and Speakers, Illustrated edition, (Grand Rapids, MI: Zondervan, 2004), p. 72.

Faith is not jumping to conclusions. It is concluding to jump. A lot of faith goes into concluding to jump out of a perfectly good airplane. Adventurists around the world put their faith in their equipment and skills just to have a momentary rush of adrenalin and euphoria. This sense of happiness is larger than life. It feels great for a short time, and then it is instantly gone. Athletes addicted to high-adrenaline activities seek out the next greatest thrill, trying to satisfy a need that only one person can completely fill.

By simply having faith the size of a tiny mustard seed, we do not have to parachute over the mountain because we can move the mountain (Matthew 17:29). It does not matter how big our faith is; rather, in Whom our faith is. By faith, we can experience a lifestyle of more than just happiness. When we believe in Jesus and are born again, we *"can rejoice with joy that is inexpressible and filled with glory"* (1 Peter 1:8 ESV). This type of joy is constant and steady, unlike happiness, which is fleeting. Joy is of the soul, which is of God, while happiness is of the moment. Someone might display happiness on the surface, but joy is within the heart. Happiness reacts while joy transcends. Happiness is based on what happens; joy is based on our journey with Jesus.

> **It does not matter how big our faith is, rather, in Whom our faith is.**

Our faith journey begins by hearing the Word, much like a skydiver hearing a parachute instructor teaching how to maneuver the steering lines and toggles (Romans 10:17). If we as children of God truly believe that His Word is *truth*, a substantial reservoir of peace and joy is availed to us. God will use His *truth* to steer us in the right direction.

What is the right direction? Being faithful. When we are faithful in the small tasks, God will entrust us with greater tasks, which brings transcending joy (Luke 16:10). There is joy when we obey the Holy

Spirit's promptings. It takes us to rewarding places. When we have an urge to apologize, perhaps we can send a smile or show sympathy. Faith makes all things possible; joy will make all things durable.

By faith, when we are headed in the right direction on our spiritual journey, joy blossoms. By faith, when we know that we are in the center of God's will, there again is joy. By faith, when we know we are fulfilling the Lord's purpose for our life, joy is found. Joy is present because His promise is being fulfilled.

This durable, inexpressible joy is proportional to our stage of faith. The great pastor to pastors, Charles Spurgeon, put it this way, "A little faith will bring your soul to heaven; a great faith will bring heaven to your soul."[21] Like jumping out of airplanes, faith takes practice. It is not hoping that God can. It is trusting that God will (Hebrews 11:1). It is not jumping to conclusions, but concluding to jump because the Creator not only packed our chute, He knit every durable fiber.

---

21   "Little Faith and Great Faith Sermon by Charles Haddon Spurgeon, November 2, 1890," The Spurgeon Library: The Spurgeon Center and Midwestern Baptist Theological Seminary, 2017, https://www.spurgeon.org/resource-library/sermons/little-faith-and-great-faith/.

Action Challenge: Exercise your faith for the next seven days:

- » Wait on God (Isaiah 40:30).
- » Rely on His strength, not yours (Ephesians 6: 10).
- » Fix your eyes on Jesus, not the news, a doctor's report, or the economy (Hebrews 12:2).
- » Listen for His small, still voice (John 10:27).

_____
_____
_____
_____
_____
_____
_____

Prayer: Father, if I can put faith in my equipment and my skills, I can certainly put my life in Your hands. Keep distractions at bay and allow me to hear the Holy Spirit's whisper clearly. In Jesus's name, amen.

> *Without faith, no joy is possible; with it, no joy is impossible.*

Day 11

Joy in Trust

Oh, the joys of those who trust the Lord...

(Psalm 40:4 NLT)

A newspaper photographer was scheduled to meet a plane on the runway to capture some aerial shots. He climbed into the first plane on the runway and said to the pilot, "Step on it!" The aviator took off and was soon in the air. The photographer asked the pilot if they could fly close to the crime scene so he could get some really good pictures. "What do you mean, take pictures?" asked the pilot. "Aren't you my flying instructor?"[22]

---

[22] "[Joke: Mistaken Flying Instructor]," Author Unknown, n.d.

Who is flying our plane? What is the picture of our trust? Choosing to trust God at our cockpit controls is the beginning and the end of a lifetime of joy. Our joy in God is bonded with our trust in God in such a way that the two cannot be divided. Trust is the spine of joy, and joy is the overflow of trust in the trustworthy One.

Throughout Scripture, trust and joy remain linked. The Psalmist speaks of the *joys of those who trust the Lord* (Psalm 40:4 NLT). Paul unites trust and joy, saying, *"May the God of hope fill you with all joy and peace in believing..."* (Romans 15:13 NIV). Even Peter connects trust and joy by explaining how we might not see Christ, but we believe in Him and rejoice with joy that is inexpressible (1 Peter 1:8). This was a hard lesson for the walk-on-water Peter, who believed he was strong enough, passionate enough, experienced enough, and loyal enough to hold onto his faith.

When the time came for Peter to stand up for Jesus, Peter denied Christ three times. In an era of social media and political correctness, we, too, can succumb to the pressure. Much like Peter, we must learn that we cannot trust in ourselves, but we must make it a lifestyle of trusting in Jesus, who is the way, the truth, and the life (John 14:6). Underline that word, *truth*. Trust starts and ends with truth. Without truth, there can be no trust, and without trust, there can be no joy.

Because Peter trusted in his strength, when asked about his relationship with Jesus, he fell. He then wept bitterly (Matthew 26:75). He felt devastated after realizing the *truth* of Jesus' words just hours prior, *"Truly, I tell you, this very night, before the rooster crows, you will deny me three times"* (Matthew 26:34 ESV).

There was no joy on Peter's journey that day. Had he only trusted in the Lord, his strength would have renewed (Isaiah 40:31). Had he trusted in Adonai's promises, his joy would have been rekindled. Even so, God does not give us what we can handle; God helps us handle what we are given. Without Jesus, disillusionment struck Peter and his trust grew thin. The state of Peter's joy was a direct outcome of the battle for his faith.

Peter could have easily remained paralyzed in his guilt, but he responded to his second calling to follow Jesus (John 21). After the resurrection, Jesus allowed Peter to start over, wiping the slate clean. After his pledge of trust, Peter became the Christian movement's first champion of sowing truth. He could finally rejoice with ineffable joy. Like Peter, we, too, can start over, trust, and live with joy.

Letting the Lord handle our plane's joysticks entails surrender-like trust, especially when we want to "step on it" and go our own way. Do not let the ariel scenery distract us from sticking to the narrow path. Jesus is the way, the truth, and the life, and He can be trusted along our journey to joy. After all, the measure of our joy is directly related to where we place our trust.

> **The measure of our joy is directly related to where we place our trust.**

Action Challenge: List at least ten experiences when Christ demonstrated His trustworthiness. File them away for when you need to be encouraged by His tried-and-true faithfulness.

_____

_____

_____

_____

_____

_____

_____

Prayer: Dear Lord, I trust in Your power to keep me, Your love to shield me, and Your wisdom to provide what is best. Teach me to trust in You at all times, even when I don't understand. In Jesus's name, amen.

Joy starts with trust and ends with trust.

Day 12

Joy in Repentance

*Purge me with hyssop, and I shall be clean;
… Let me hear joy and gladness…*

(Psalm 51:7–8 ESV)

A police officer pulled over a driver and alerted him that because he was wearing a seat belt, he had just won $1,000 in a safety competition. "What are you going to do with the prize money?" the officer asked. The man responded, "I guess I'll go to driving school and get my license." At that moment, his wife, who was seated next to him, chimed in, "Officer, don't listen to him. He's a smarty when he's drunk." This woke up the guy in the back seat, who, when he saw the cop, blurted out, "I knew we wouldn't get far in this stolen car." At that moment, there was a knock from the trunk, and a voice asked, "Are we over the border yet?" [23]

---

[23] "131+ Listen Jokes and Funny Puns," JokoJokes, Accessed January 28, 2024, https://jokojokes.com/listen-jokes.html.

This story gives greater meaning to taxicab confessions. Many people confess when it is not the offense but the penalty that troubles them. Regardless of why humans instinctively feel the need to confess or admit their wrongdoing, the urge to confess is a cop's best friend. More importantly, we become a friend of God when we confess our sins to Him. He promises that He is faithful and just to forgive us of our sins and to cleanse us (1 John 1:9). It is also important that we confess our sins to one another so that we *"may be healed"* and freed from guilt (James 5:16 NIV).

Freedom from guilt begins with confession and ends with repentance. Repentance (turning from the world's way to God's way) hinges upon confession. We cannot repent when we have not first admitted wrongdoing. Repentance means we change our minds so deeply that it changes us.

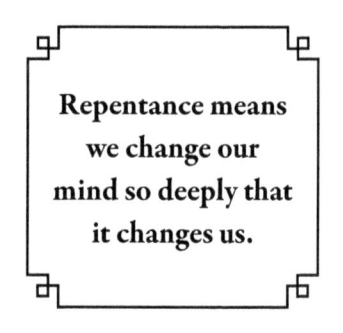

> **Repentance means we change our mind so deeply that it changes us.**

Change comes with a deep sense of brokenness. That grief leads to true repentance and produces divine joy. The very moment we stop on our journey, admit we are wrong, and commit to change, God leaps for joy... then so do we (Luke 15:7).

Consider when David disobeyed God; his joy vanished. The only way to restore his joy was by true repentance. He prayed, *"Cleanse me with hyssop, and I will be clean ... Let me hear joy and gladness..."* (Psalm 51:7–8 NIV). With sin blocking the pathway, joy was impossible. David became so miserable from committing murder and adultery that the weight of sin and guilt physically crushed him, *"...my bones wasted away through my groaning all day long"* (Psalm 32:3 NIV). He could not escape the pressure until he confessed his sins to God. He did not just show remorse but reversal.

When he spoke of being purged with hyssop, David did not see it as a cleansing or healing agent. It was only the instrument for applying the cleansing agent. He had in mind the blood of the Passover lamb that turned away God's wrath (Exodus 12:22) or the water-blood mixture that ceremonially cleansed the defiled (Leviticus 14:4–7). David's request to be purged with hyssop meant that God would dip the plant into the sacrificial blood and apply it to his heart to be restored with joy (Psalm 51:12).

Today, we do not have to confess via ritual practices or routine traffic stops; we can go straight to a Holy God who will cleanse us. Buckle up and embrace a lifestyle of repentance to keep our tank full of joy. If we want progress, and yet we are on the wrong road, that means making a U-turn and driving back to the right road, in which case, the person who turns back soonest is the most progressive. After all, we cannot repent too soon since we cannot know how soon is too late.

Action Challenge: On an electronic device, take time to write down every area where you need repentance and restoration, then confess to God, and delete them as if they never even existed.

_____

_____

_____

_____

_____

_____

_____

Prayer: Heavenly Father, wash me thoroughly from my iniquity. I plead for Your cleansing forgiveness over me because of Your finished work of redemption on the cross. In Jesus's name, amen.

To be full of sin is to be empty of God's joy.
To be empty of sin is to be full of God's joy.

Day 13

Joy in Faithfulness

His master said to him, "Well done, good and faithful servant. You have been faithful over a little; I will set you over much. Enter into the joy of your master."

(Matthew 25:21 ESV)

For months, [Rusty] had been [Rachel's] devoted admirer. Now, at long last, he had collected up sufficient courage to ask her the most momentous of all questions, "There are quite a lot of advantages to being a bachelor," [Rusty] began, "but there comes a time when one longs for the companionship of another being––a being who will regard one as perfect, as a role model; whom one can treat as one's absolute own; who will be kind and faithful when times are hard; who will share one's joys and sorrows." To his delight, [Rusty] saw a sympathetic gleam in [Rachel's] eyes. Then she nodded in agreement.

Finally, she responded, "I think it's a great idea! Can I help you choose which puppy to buy?"[24]

---

24   Pastor Tim, "Puppy Love," The Cybersalt Site, Accessed January 28, 2024, https://www.cybersalt.org/clean-jokes/puppy-love.

Ouch! Did she really say that out loud? Thorns may hurt us, people may disappoint us, and sunlight may turn to fog, but we are never friendless even if we have a dog. Roger Caras once said, "Dogs are not our whole life, but they make our lives whole."[25] Imagine if we came with that same level of faithfulness in our relationships with God and others; our lives really could be made whole. Why? Because faithfulness is the key that opens the door to the joy of the Lord.

Jesus used the familiar picture of a master and servant to teach the disciples about the principle of remaining faithful to what God has called us to do, *"Blessed is that servant whom his master will find so doing when he comes"* (Matthew 24:46 ESV). As servants of God, we will be blessed if He finds us faithful upon Jesus' return. We will not only be blessed to hear the words, *"Well done, good and faithful servant,"* we will be blessed to experience the joy of our Master (Matthew 25:21 ESV). The fruit of faithfulness is joy since *joy* and *faithfulness* are both fruits of the Holy Spirit.

> *Jesus doesn't just call us to be faithful, He generates faithfulness in us by the Spirit. With the Spirit's help, we can be faithful stewards of our resources (1 Corinthians 4:2), be faithful in our truthfulness (2 Corinthians 1:18), be faithful in our suffering (1 Peter 4:19), [and be faithful to the point of death (Revelation 2:10)].*[26]

---

25 "A Quote by Roger A. Caras," Goodreads, 2024, https://www.goodreads.com/quotes/19168-dogs-are-not-our-whole-life-but-they-make-our.
26 Rondi Lauterbach, "Faithfulness: A Promise That Leads to Joy," Rondi Lauterbach (blog), March 16, 2021, https://www.rondilauterbach.com/2021/03/16/faithfulness-a-promise-that-leads-to-joy/.

When we are faithful in little things, God will give us the opportunity to be faithful over greater things. Faithfulness in little things is, therefore, a **huge** thing. In other words, ordinary faithfulness leads to extraordinary joy. While there is no right way to do wrong, there is no wrong way to do right. Faithfulness is not doing the right thing one time but doing the right thing all the time. When we make it a lifestyle of doing right over and over and over, we will create for ourselves a lifetime of joy.

Does a lifetime of joy seem too far out of reach? Does the idea of doing right over and over seem too *dog*matic? Or on a short leash because God cannot trust us in the small things? If a puppy can show loyalty in return for dinner scraps, why can't we show faithfulness in return for His daily feast? When the Lord reprimands us to reverse course and get back on the narrow track, our journey will turn to joy. After all, faithfulness is our constant joy; fruitfulness is God's.

Action Challenge: Journal five key areas in which you can become more faithful to God, your family, or friends... then do it (i.e., follow through with even the little promises you make to your kids and the rest of your family; they are the biggest test to our faith).

_____
_____
_____
_____
_____
_____
_____

Prayer: Heavenly Father, You have called me to be faithful in the little things. Thank you for being faithful to me even when I am not faithful to You. May Your Spirit rain down so I might have power to live a lifestyle of faithfulness until Jesus returns. In Jesus' name, amen.

Our joy is not in the truthfulness of our own knowing but in the faithfulness of the One who's known.

Day 14

Joy in Obedience

If you keep my commandments ... my joy may be in you, and that your joy may be full.

(John 15:10–11 ESV)

A young boy was having a conversation with his mom one day when he proudly boasted about how he and his father took a journey on the bus just that morning, "Dad told me to give up my seat to a beautiful lady." Of course, the Mom beamed with excitement because her little boy would obey his father and **do** *the right thing by giving up his seat. However, her son leaned over and whispered in her ear, "My seat was Daddy's lap!"*[27]

---

27 Gerry Hopman, Kids Say the "Doggonest" Things, (USA: G. H. Hopman and Associates Ltd., 2005), p. 51.

Just because we have the right to do something does not make it the right thing to do (1 Corinthians 10:13). Just because it may be legal does not make it moral. Throughout Israel's history, the Israelites turned away from God time and again, developing their customs and definitions of morality. Because of their disobedience, God scattered them. For nearly a millennium, the Hebrews lacked joy as they lived apart from the Law and God.

However, God promised to bring a remnant back to Jerusalem to rebuild the kingdom for His people (Isaiah 10–11; Jeremiah 31). Around 444 B.C., God fulfilled this promise. The Israelites returned to Jerusalem and built the wall and a new temple. During the dedication, Ezra gathered all the people and brought out a copy of the Scriptures that had been lost for 1,000 years. When Ezra began to read the law aloud, the people savored every moment and pleaded to stay and listen for the next eight days. To them, they were stunned by this long-lost treasure, now re-discovered.

During their marathon revival, the Jews learned how the Children of Israel were to dwell in booths during the feasts of the seventh month. This was a challenge to their obedience, for they *"had not done so"* since Joshua's time (Nehemiah 8:17 ESV). They had not observed the feasts during the period of the kings or the prophets, yet they finally came across this duty that they needed to practice. These folks came with such a naïve simplicity of the Word of God that they concluded, "God said we should be sitting in huts and observing the feasts, why don't we do that? When do we start? Let's go get the sticks and get the huts built." It was a eureka moment! They did not understand why, but because God had said it, they needed to obey it. They turned a Holy Day into a holiday.

The Hebrews became more than just hearers of the Word, but doers (James 1:22). Because of their obedience, their weeping turned to joy. Nehemiah 8:10 (NIV) went on to proclaim, *"This day is holy to our Lord. Do not grieve, for the joy of the Lord is your*

> A ton of prayer or Scripture reading will not produce what an ounce of obedience will.

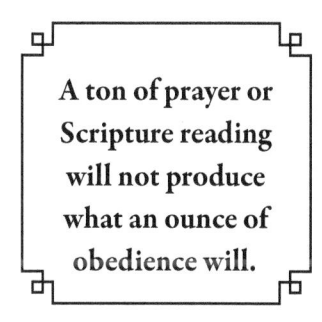

strength." So, they celebrated with great joy (Nehemiah 8:12).

A ton of prayer or Scripture reading will not produce what an ounce of obedience will. This is why Jesus made clear that if we keep His commandments, our joy will be full (John 15:11). He links obedience and joy in a cause-and-effect manner, meaning joy results from obedience. Only those who are obedient—who pursue a lifestyle of holiness—will experience a lifetime of joy.

"When the law of God is written in our hearts, our duty will be our delight."[28] Obedience to God is the pathway to the life we really want to live, even if it means offering our seats on the bus. People of character do the right thing even if no one else does, not because they think it will change the world but because they refuse to be changed by the world (Romans 12:2). They remain obedient.

---

28   "Quote by Matthew Henry," Grace Quotes, 2024, https://gracequotes.org/author-quote/matthew-henry/.

Action Challenge: Take an Eight-Day Hebrew Challenge to read through biblical duties not just meant to be heard but done. Praise Him (Psalm 63:3), be morally pure (1 Corinthians 6:18–20), give generously (2 Corinthians 9:13), shine your light (Matthew 5:16), care for the orphans and widows (James 1:27), etc. Then, see your joy increase.

___

___

___

___

___

___

___

___

Prayer: Dear Father, please teach me to value, consume, and obey Your holy written Word. Lord, allow Your joy to become my strength as I grow into a lifelong student of the Bible. In Jesus's name, amen.

Perfect obedience would equal perfect joy if only we had perfect trust in the Person we are obeying.

Day 15

Joy in Salvation

Yet I will rejoice in the LORD; I will take joy in the God of my salvation.

(Habakkuk 3:18 ESV)

After failing to climb Mount Everest, John ended with severe frostbite and hypothermia, forcing him into a coma. Mercifully, a heroic rescue team saved John on the mountaintop. They rushed him to a hospital where, after four days, he finally awoke and greeted a Nepalese doctor. The physician smiled and explained to John that he had good news and bad news, to which John-the-optimist asked for the good news first. "Okay," replied the surgeon, "the good news is that the patient in the next bed has offered you a very generous amount for your mountaineering boots..."[29]

---

[29] "Everest Jokes - 77 Hilarious Everest Jokes," Upjoke.com, Accessed January 29, 2024, https://upjoke.com/everest-jokes.

In salvation, there is always good news because it is sourced in the Gospel's Good News. For earthly salvation, God uses rescued people to rescue people, yet for eternal salvation, God uses no one other than Jesus Christ (Acts 4:12). He is on the journey to rescue people from misery to everlasting joy, which can only be found in Him. There is no salvation without surrender, no life without death, and no joy without Jesus.

> **For earthly salvation, God uses rescued people to rescue people, yet for eternal salvation God uses no one else other than Jesus Christ.**

Throughout Scripture, salvation and joy go together. In Luke 15, Jesus tells the stories of the lost coin, the prodigal son, and the lost sheep being found. At the end of each illustration, there was tremendous joy. The prophet Habakkuk also connected salvation with joy (Habakkuk 3:18). He went on to explain that when met with losses and crosses in the world, Christians can still praise the Lord as the God of their salvation because of the hope of a heavenly crown. In this, we are reminded to hold onto our earthly possessions and comforts loosely.

When the angels announced Christ's birth, they revealed that a Savior was coming who would bring *"good news of great joy"* (Luke 2:10 ESV). Peter also connected joy with salvation, *"you greatly rejoice with joy inexpressible and full of glory"* (1 Peter 1:8 NASB). In each example, joy is a result of God's gift of salvation. Those of us who are saved should experience that level of joy. We must *"rejoice always,"* as Paul urged (1 Thessalonians 5:16 NIV). Why? Since joy and rejoicing are elements within the saving work of our Lord.

As believers, Jesus is our built-in mechanism for continual joy. Conversely, when sin enters the journey, joy departs. David faced that dilemma after committing adultery and murder as he cried out,

"Restore to me the joy of your salvation..." (Psalm 51:12 ESV). He hungered to relive the joyful moments when he experienced salvation and unblemished fellowship with his savior.

Just as David traveled down a path toward destruction, so can we. Accordingly, we can resume the Journey in Joy when we make it a lifestyle to greet God with a surrendered heart and set our affections on things above (Colossians 3:2). Peter clarifies it further by advising how we can restore the joy of our salvation by anticipating the protected inheritance that every one of us has in Christ (1 Peter 1:4). The full inheritance can never perish, never be disqualified, and never fade away. In this, we should be jubilant!

There is often joy in the anticipation of what is to come. There are times when the anticipation is better than the main event. However, this will not be true for our eternal home. To experience mountaintop joy, we must keep our eyes on the protected inheritance.

Action Challenge: Write down the joy you felt when accepting Jesus. Recall this memory in tough times. If you need salvation, ask forgiveness for your sins, be willing to turn from your sins, and believe that Jesus Christ—our Lord and Savior—died for your sins and rose again. Talk it over with another believer.

_____

_____

_____

_____

_____

_____

_____

Prayer: Jesus, only You "can turn a mess into a message, a test into a testimony, a trial into a triumph, a victim into a victor," and a dive into a divine rescue.[30] I am grateful for the joy of Your salvation. In Jesus' name, amen.

> *To be a Christian without joy is no more possible than to be alive without breathing or be saved without a Savior.*

---

[30] "Quote by Fern Bernstein: Mah Jongg Mondays: A Memoir about Friendship, Love, and Faith," Goodreads, Inc., Accessed January 29, 2024, https://www.goodreads.com/quotes/10353137-only-god-can-turn-a-mess-into-a-message-a.

Day 16

Joy in Assurance

...rejoice that your names are written in heaven.

(Luke 10:20 NIV)

A pastor boarded an airplane to take his first flight ever. Just before take-off, the flight attendant noticed his clerical garb and panicked face, his white knuckles gripping the seat in semi-terror. She walked over to the reverend, saying, "Sir, you are a man of faith—you shouldn't be so nervous about flying. Don't you have faith in God?" The cleric looked up and said, "Ma'am, the assurance in Scripture is, 'Lo, I am with you always.' It doesn't say anything about 'height.'"[31]

---

31 Michael Hodgin, 1001 More Humorous Illustrations for Public Speaking: Fresh, Timely, and Compelling Illustrations for Preachers, Teachers, and Speakers, (Grand Rapids, MI: Zondervan, 1998), p. 414.

There will always be highs and lows on our journey in this life; we can be assured of that. Also, we are also assured that our salvation is secure (Romans 8:1). It is not a "hope so" but a "know so" salvation. Deep joy is rooted in the confidence that we are saved. No matter how tough things become, we can know with absolute certainty where we will spend eternity (1 John 5:13). When he faced assassination plots, Paul did not cry out, "Woe is me!" Rather, he longed to be *absent from the body* and present with the Lord (2 Corinthians 5:8 KJV). He found great joy and surety in his future, following the prompt of Luke that all who believe should rejoice knowing our *"...names are written in heaven"* (Luke 10:20 NIV).

> **It is not a 'hope so' but a 'know so' salvation.**

The more we travel our winding journey here, the more we long for our eternal home. When life is good and everything is going well, we may not dwell on our eternal home so much. However, when life seems out of control, or we have lost our way, we long for our eternal home. The reason believers have joy is that we know that the moment we pass from this life, there is an ethereal dwelling waiting for us in all its splendor. Jesus promised in Heaven, there will be no evil, death, or pain. It is a real place where the streets are paved with gold, the gates are made of pearl, and the walls are embedded with precious gems (Revelation 21).

Can we know for sure we are heaven-bound with salvation sealed? Yes. Scripture teaches that when a person admits to their sin, asks God for forgiveness, and accepts forgiveness through the saving work of the risen Christ, God appoints His Spirit to come into our lives as a preserving seal to forever lock in our faith. The authenticating seal serves to validate our citizenship in Heaven. When we believed, we were marked in Him with a seal guaranteeing our inheritance (Ephesians 1:13–14).

Without the real assurance of salvation as a bedrock, it is tricky for a new Christian to grow and experience the deeper blessings of the Christian life. Neglect of worship, fellowship, and prayer are all thieves that weaken our assurance and steal our joy. Let us understand that even though our assurance may waiver, our salvation never will (Romans 8:38–39; John 10:28). Salvation is fixed as a true believer. By practicing a lifestyle of spiritual disciplines in our lives, our assurance of salvation strengthens while our joy proportionally grows.

Before boarding, be assured that God is in control. No matter how high or low our journey goes or how white our knuckles clutch, there is joy in knowing our salvation is secure. If God is all we have, we have all we need (John 14:8). We may not know what the future holds, yet we know Who holds the future. Maybe that is why so few atheists are found on turbulent airplanes.

Action Challenge: When you come to a stressful moment, find an ointment for your fears, anxieties, bitterness, resentment, or helplessness by imagining the spectacular beauty of Heaven filled with angelic song and the glorious presence of the Lord. Envision your salvation is secured in the blissful brilliance of paradise.

_____

_____

_____

_____

_____

_____

_____

Prayer: Lord, thank you for Your blessed assurance that stirs our expectant joy of Your return. May Your peace and confidence permeate all our lives as we live for You. In Jesus' name, amen.

Joy is the sealed assurance that you are Kingdom-bound.

Day 17

Joy in Gratitude

> How can we give God enough thanks for you for all the joy you give us?
>
> (1 Thessalonians 3:9 NLV)

John's family gave him a rescue parrot as a gift, whose attitude was bad with an even worse vocabulary. Every word was rude and laced with profanity. John tried many different ways to stop the parrot from cursing, but nothing worked. Exasperated, he grabbed the bird and threw it into the freezer... just for a minute. Realizing his error, John swiftly opened the freezer only to have the parrot calmly step out onto his arm, saying, "I believe I may have offended you with my rude language, sir. I'm sincerely sorry and thankful to be adopted into your home." All made sense when the bird whispered, "May I ask what the turkey did?"[32]

---

[32] "'Attitude' Adjustment," Hot Springs Sentinel Record, September 19, 2021, https://www.hotsr.com/news/2021/sep/19/attitude-adjustment/.

We do not have to be a frozen Thanksgiving turkey before discovering how blessed we truly are. Whether rich or poor, healthy or unhealthy, just or unjust, a believer or nonbeliever, we all can experience and appreciate undeserved blessings from God (Matthew 5:45). His common grace allows everyone the opportunity to taste a sliver of spontaneous joy, such as laughter with one another or the aroma of sweet honeysuckle. Blissful moments like these are mere gifts meant to point to an extraordinary Lord.

Being grateful is hard enough when life is good because we tend to take for granted our conveniences, comforts, and curing… like the nine ungrateful lepers (Luke 17:15–17). When life is tough, it is tough to be thankful. Despite his solitude and suffering, Paul chose to rejoice always and give thanks in all circumstances (1 Thessalonians 5:16, 18). Notice that the apostle did not give thanks *for* all circumstances but *in* all circumstances. Because of his utter appreciation for God's grace *in* the hard times, Paul asks, *"How can we give God enough thanks for you for all the joy you give us?"* (1 Thessalonians 3:9 NLV). Other biblical examples of appreciation include Daniel, who gave thanks despite the risk of death (Daniel 6:10). Jonah gave thanks in the belly of a fish (Jonah 2:9). David gave thanks in the face of deep injustice (Psalm 69:4).

Gratitude is a counterpoint to times of defeat, unreached aspirations, and profound disappointments. It is a counterpoint when we desire more than what God has called us to have. Why? Because we do not need more to be thankful for, we just need to be more thankful for what He has given. Thank Him for all He has given, both big and small. As a result of this authentic appreciation, God will afford His common grace of joy. An ungrateful spirit, however, leads to the opposite effect. A sense of entitlement bubbles up because it is rooted in self. When we do not get what we think we "deserve," envy turns into complaining, which robs us of our joy. For joy to live in our life, something must die in our life. That "something" is selfishness.

When selflessness replaces selfishness, humility is born in the heart so that the magnitude of our gratitude can brighten our attitude. Such resulting joy might be the best positive reinforcement to stop us from parroting offensive words... cold turkey. More than likely, though, it will take a lifestyle of giving thanks in all things along life's journey. Doing so might not change the situation, but it will change us in the situation. We change because our perspective changes. We change because gratitude unlocks our hearts for God to remind us that we are adopted into His home where the fullness of joy may be experienced. Scientific research shows what Scripture already told us: gratitude makes us joyful. When we develop a lifestyle of thankfulness, our hearts become filled with joy (Philippians 1:3–5).

> **For joy to live in our life, something must die in our life. That 'something' is selfishness.**

Action Challenge: God gave you a gift of 84,600 seconds today. Have you used one to say thank you? Over the next forty days, journal three things each day you are grateful for, starting with His forgiveness of your sins and saving grace.

_____
_____
_____
_____
_____
_____
_____

Prayer: God, this is the day that You have made; I will rejoice and be glad in it. I thank you for preserving my life today and for the many days I have been given. I am grateful for Christ's sacrifice so that my sins are forgiven. In Jesus' name, amen.

Gratitude transforms our attitude to joy.

Day 18

Joy in Humility

The humble will be filled with fresh joy from the LORD.

(Isaiah 29:19a NLT)

Being around children, we've all probably heard some pretty funny things, much like a boy who was effortlessly skipping stones across the pond with his father when he said, "Dad, how does it feel to have a perfect human being for a son?" Without hesitation, the father replied, "I don't know son, ask your grandpa." [33]

---

[33] "[Anecdote: Boy Asks Dad How It Feels to Have a Perfect Son.," Author Unknown, n.d.

Like father like son. Except that is precisely the point. The son should very much be like the Father. When we see the Son of God in relationship to the Heavenly Father, we see the greatest example of humility from Jesus, *"Who, as He already existed in the form of God, did not consider equality with God something to be grasped, but emptied Himself..."* (Philippians 2:6–7 NASB). No one had to humble Him. He humbled Himself, dying on the cross for our sins, the humblest act imaginable.

Since Jesus illustrates perfect humility, true joy comes from having the mind of Christ that puts others first. We are to make our *"...joy complete by being like-minded, having the same love, being one in spirit and of one mind. Do nothing out of selfish ambition or vain conceit. Rather, in humility value others above yourselves"* (Philippians 2:2–3 NIV). When we think like Jesus, we will become like Jesus, who always puts others over Himself. Plus, when we clothe ourselves in humility, *"...we will be filled with fresh joy from the LORD"* (Isaiah 29:19 NLT).

The opposite is also true. As imperfect creatures, pride often steals our joy because pride is rooted in self, the antithesis of humility. Many theologians claim that pride is the root cause of all our sins. When satan rebelled against God, taking one-third of all the angels with him, pride won. When Adam and Eve ate the forbidden fruit, thinking they could become equal with God, pride won. When King David thought he could get away with an affair with Bathsheba, pride won. When we are preoccupied with our self-image, pride wins. When we brag about how *un*materialistic we are, pride wins. When we feel morally superior, pride wins. When we are unteachable, pride wins.

Even when we try to be humble, we often make it all about us. When we try to deflect compliments, we may be demonstrating pride because we are more concerned about how we look to others instead of responding with grace. Either way, we must guard ourselves from

> "Humility is not thinking less of yourself, it's thinking of yourself less."
>
> - Rick Warren

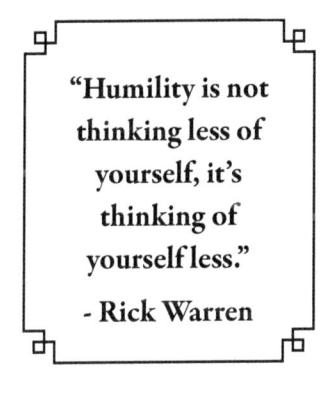

denying our strengths and being too honest about our weaknesses. Rick Warren said it well, "Humility is not thinking less of yourself, it is thinking of yourself less."[34] Indeed, *"God resists the proud, but gives grace to the humble"* (1 Peter 5:5b NKJV). It is by this grace that we become filled with joy.

Before we cast any stones, we must examine our pride before the Lord (John 8:7). The pathway to experiencing fresh joy through humility is in making a lifestyle of espousing the same attitude as Christ, the only perfect human ever to walk this earth. It is not a place of weakness but a high road of strength that allows us to travel gracefully, empowering others to join us on the journey.

---

[34] Rick Warren, The Purpose Driven Life, First Edition, (Zondervan, 2002).

Action Challenge: Ask the Holy Spirit to teach you one way you can be humble. Do it and keep it private!

_____
_____
_____
_____
_____
_____
_____
_____

Prayer: Dear Lord Jesus, when I contemplate how You, the King of Glory, left Your heavenly throne and humbled Yourself to bear the wretchedness of this life, my pride disgusts me. Forgive my arrogance and help me to take Your hand as You lead me where You have been before––into the valley of humility and selfless service. Please give me a teachable spirit and a heart fresh with joy as I journey with you. In Jesus' name, amen.

> *They that know God will be humble; they that know pride know not joy.*

Day 19

Joy in Contentment

I rejoiced greatly in the Lord ... I have learned the secret of being content in any and every situation...

(Philippians 4:10, 12 NIV)

A woman woke up one morning looking in the mirror, only to see she had three hairs left on her head. "Great," she said, "I think I'll braid my hair today." The next day, she woke up, looked in the mirror, and saw that she had only two hairs on her head. "Hmm," she said, "I guess I'll part my hair down the middle." The next day, she woke up, looked in the mirror, and saw that she had only one hair. "Wow," she said, "today I get to wear my hair in a ponytail." The next day, she woke up, looked in the mirror, and saw that there wasn't a single hair on her head. "Thank God!" she rejoiced. "I was running out of things to do with my hair!"[35]

---

[35] Mary Hollingsworth, The One Year Devotional of Joy and Laughter: 365 Inspirational Meditations to Brighten Your Day, (Carol Stream, IL: Tyndale House Publishers, 2011), p. 11.

We cannot control everything. Our hair is a reminder of that. However, what we can control is our state of contentment. Being content means being satisfied and believing we have enough. It is an inner sense of rest or peace that comes from being right with God and trusting that He is in control of everything that happens.

Intriguingly, the root word for contentment evolves from the Latin word "contentus," meaning "held together," "intact," or "whole."[36] Initially, "contentus" represented containers such as cups or clay pots. Later, the word grew into a meaning that projected upon individuals, describing people who feel complete and whole. To live a life of contentment may seem lofty, yet to experience joy from that contentment may seem downright impossible.

By God's grace, the Apostle Paul demonstrated to us that finding joy in contentment *is* possible. Contentment was not concession; it was satisfaction (Hebrews 13:5–6). Despite living a life of hardship and persecution during every step of his journey, Paul paid little attention to those afflictions yet secretly found contentment in a prison cell. What satisfied him most was the joy he had in Jesus. He needed nothing else outside of rejoicing in the Lord, *"...whether well fed or hungry, whether living in plenty or in want"* (Philippians 4:12 NIV).

The encounter Paul had with Christ on his journey to Damascus taught him how satisfaction did not come by putting to death those who knew Christ, yet it was *knowing* Christ and putting to death ego that brought satisfaction (Mark 8:35). Having fewer things less self and less pride meant more Jesus. Paul learned when he was most satisfied in God, God was most glorified in him.

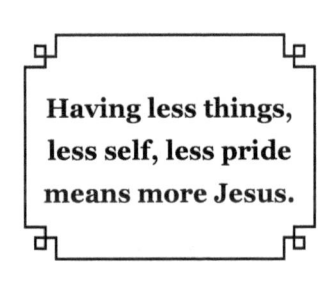

> **Having less things, less self, less pride means more Jesus.**

---

[36] "Contentment," Etymology of contentment by etymonline, 2024, https://www.etymonline.com/word/contentment.

Early on, Paul conceded how comparison steals joy. He knew a desire for wealth beyond basic necessities did not lead to more contentment because material wealth has no eternal value. After all, we brought nothing into the world, and we can take nothing out of it (1 Timothy 6:7).

An elderly man finally learned this, confessing it to a group of friends, "I was dying to finish high school so that I could go to college, and then I was dying to finish college so I could start my career, and then I was dying to get married so that I could have a family, and then I was dying for my kids to turn 18 so that they could leave, and then I was dying to retire ... and now that I'm retired, I'm just dying." [37]

When we are dying for that next widget, next promotion, next hairstyle, next thing, we are no longer living for Christ. Paul insisted that a lifestyle of godliness may not lead to financial gain, but it does restore our joy and contentment, which is the greatest treasure we could ever acquire. The most precious things in life are not really things.

---

37 Tony Evans, Tony Evans' Book of Illustrations: Stories, Quotes, and Anecdotes from More Than 30 Years of Preaching and Public Speaking, New edition. (Chicago, IL: Moody Publishers, 2009).

Action Challenge: Collect those personal items you no longer need and donate them to a local charity. Free up the clutter in your life to make room for your joy of satisfaction in God.

___

___

___

___

___

___

___

Prayer: Yahweh, You alone are my inheritance, my cup of blessing that can overflow with joy. I know this, yet I am constantly tempted by the material things of this world. Help me resist covetousness and find contentment in Jesus alone. Give me only what brings glory to You. In Jesus' name, amen.

Collect joyous moments with God, not things of man.

Day 20

Joy in Forgiveness

Oh, what joy for those whose disobedience is forgiven, whose sin is put out of sight!

(Psalms 32:1 NLT)

A couple flying to their vacation destination endured an emergency landing on an uncharted island beach. The odds of rescue were slim. Hours after surviving the harrowing incident, Don asked his wife Julie if she had paid their $5,000 in taxes, but she shook her head no. He then asked her if she had paid their Visa card, but again, she shook her head no. Finally, he asked Julie if their monthly church tithe was paid, to which she said, "Oh, Don, will you ever forgive me? I did not pay that one either." At just that moment, Don grabbed Julie, giving her a celebratory kiss and the warmest embrace in forty years. She pried him away, asking him what in the world was going on. With great joyfulness in his breath, Don bellowed, "They'll find us, they'll find us!"[38]

---

[38] "Travel at 60 Daily Joke: A Husband and Wife Are Flying to Australia," Starts at 60, January 27, 2019, https://startsat60.com/media/travel/husband-wife-joke-flying-australia-crash-landing.

On our journey in joy, there will be system failures and emergency landings, whether due to our mistakes or someone else's. King David made his fair share of mistakes like adultery and murder, overwhelming him with substantial guilt. He felt like he was on a deserted island where his *"body wasted away,"* and he groaned *"all day long"* (Psalm 32:3 NLT). His strength *"evaporated like water in the summer heat"* (Psalm 32:4 NLT). Forgiveness became David's eject button from all the guilt that was stealing his joy.

Once the king took responsibility for his sin, admitted his guilt before God, and pleaded for forgiveness, the psalmist could sing, "Oh, what joy for those whose disobedience is forgiven" (Psalms 32:1 NLT). David's epiphany came when forgiveness rescued him from God's wrath. Paul incorporated Psalm 32's deep truth into Romans 4:7 (HCSB), "How joyful are those whose lawless acts are forgiven and whose sins are covered!" With so much joy to experience when we fully grasp how all our debt has been paid, we will want to give the Heavenly Father the warmest embrace ever. He will "find us" alright; it begins when He captains our flight.

When we confess and surrender to the Lord to pilot our journey, joy will overflow from all the celestial celebration. *"...there will be more rejoicing in heaven over one sinner who repents than over ninety-nine righteous persons who do not need to repent"* (Luke 15:7 NIV). Forgiveness does not stop at the gates of Heaven; it continues in our earthly relationships. We are to forgive each other just as the Lord has forgiven us (Colossians 3:13). The ethereal joy of forgiving and being forgiven crystallizes a euphoria that is out of this world.

> **When we confess and surrender to the Lord to pilot our journey, joy will overflow from all the celestial celebration.**

Forgiveness is a function of the heart and soul that closes anger's door and opens joy's floodgate. Once our gushing joy is received, we should feel eager to live a lifestyle of forgiving ourselves and others. After all, forgiven people forgive people. Though forgiveness does not change the past, it does change the future with joy by freeing us from the control of those who harm us. Understanding, empathy, and compassion often follow. While on the cross, Christ modeled this for us when He wept, *"Father, forgive them, for they know not what they do"* (Luke 23:34 ESV).

As believers, we have the supernatural ability to forgive others perpetually (Matthew 18:22). Why? Because in Christ, we have everything we need for joy–the forgiveness of sins, the Holy Spirit's indwelling, a purpose for living, and the assurance of salvation... no matter the debt we owe. He has already paid it (Colossians 2:14). We can choose to board *Anger Flight 666,* which cycles nonstop and crashes, or we can choose to board *Forgiveness Flight 777* bound for angelic joy because sin is "put out of sight."

Action Challenge: Ask God for forgiveness. Discern where resentment is hidden. Practice empathy. Try seeing the situation from the other person's point of view; choose to forgive them.

_____

_____

_____

_____

_____

_____

_____

Prayer: O Lord, please forgive my failings and equip me to forgive others. Thank you for clearing my debt and rescuing me from the deserted island I was on. In Jesus' name, amen.

The joy of forgiveness is when justice and grace kiss.

Day 21

Joy in Love

[Jesus said,] ... My joy may be in you and your joy may be full. ... "Love each other just as I have loved you."

(John 15:11–12 NLV)

An elderly couple traveled to Israel, where the wife died suddenly of a heart attack. A local mortician tried to ease the husband's concerns, explaining he could pay $100 to bury his wife in Israel rather than $3,000 to send her back to America. After a few moments of thinking, the husband informed the mortician that he would like to have his wife transported home despite the insistence of the incredulous mortician. The older visitor explained himself, "I've heard of a guy who died and was buried here many years ago, and he came back after three days. I'm not going to risk that!"[39]

---

[39] "A Man Goes on Vacation to Israel with His Wife and His Stepmother," Reddit Post, R/Jokes, August 17, 2018, www.reddit.com/r/Jokes/comments/982rbu/a_man_goes_on_vacation_to_israel_with_his_wife/.

Perhaps the aged American was thinking much like Linus VanPelt from Peanuts, who quipped, "I [We all] love mankind... It's people I [we] can't stand!"[40] Whether or not we can stand certain people along our life's path, we are still commanded to make it a daily practice to "love each other" just as Jesus has loved us (John 15:11–12). When Jesus spoke these words, He was in the Upper Room on the night of His betrayal and arrest. He knew what was next, and He did not want His disciples to lose their joy. Jesus comforted them, "...be of good cheer, I have overcome the world" (John 16:33 KJV). His inner joy was the same joy that gave Him the strength to endure the excruciating suffering of His crucifixion, His great act of love for us. It is this very same joy God intends for us to have as we exercise the love of Christ. Full joy fuels our love for one another and comes from loving one another.

Where the world believes that true joy is found in selfish living, those who believe in Christ see what emptiness this lifestyle brings. The message of loving others may sound counter-intuitive, and it certainly is counter-cultural, yet when we commit to loving each other through the power of the Holy Spirit, it comes from the overflow of joy in God that meets people's needs. Just because we are called to love our enemies or those who are hard to love, that does not mean we have to endorse their actions.

> **Just because we are called to love our enemies or those who are hard to love, that does not mean we have to endorse their actions.**

"Loving your neighbor as yourself" does not spawn intangible fairy dust that magically inspires us to do good because God is love (Mark 12:31). This command is about how we are to treat one another, meet other's needs, and put others concerns above our own. This can be

---

40   "Quote by Charles Shultz," My Geek Wisdom (blog), September 4, 2021, https://mygeekwisdom.com/2021/09/04/i-love-mankind-its-people-i-cant-stand/.

done when the joy and love we have in God fills us to the brim, and we can pour over into others' lives. Paul perfectly exemplified this. Every time Paul spoke about his joy in his friends, he also referred to his joy in Christ. Ultimately, his delight in people came out of his delight in Jesus. Put differently, Paul did not seek to love in order to be joyful. He sought to be joyful in God in order to spill forth God's love, for God is love.

When we love others, joy will follow (Philemon 1:7). But will others want to follow Christ because of our love for them? No matter where we travel on our journey, locally or around the world, we will encounter those who are simply hard to love. And yet, we are called to make a lifestyle of loving them; sharing the Good News of salvation so that one day they might reach the Promised Land. Yes, joy can be found in the Lord's Son, who died and was buried in Israel many years ago. After three days, He did not just come back; he rose from the dead and defeated death. He was the sacrificial lamb so we could have joy in all things. This was the greatest display of love (John 15:13). Does His joy and love remain in us to make our joy full?

Action Challenge: Make a concerted effort today to seek out a person who needs your love and joy. Grace them with kind words and even kinder deeds. Respond with gentleness (Proverbs 15:1).

_____
_____
_____
_____
_____
_____
_____

Prayer: Loving God, fill me with Your love, bringing joy and peace. May my sacrificial love overflow to others. Keep my heart pure and my faith passionate. In Jesus' name, amen.

Joy is not a goal… it's a by-product of a lifestyle of love.

Day 22

Joy in Service

Make a joyful noise to the Lord, all the earth! Serve the LORD with gladness!

(Psalm 100:1–2 ESV)

Road trips are great fun until the journey interferes with other life happenings, like attending Uncle Charlie's memorial service. William just couldn't make it, so he instructed his brother, "Do something nice to pay it forward for Uncle Charlie, and then send me the bill!" Later, William got a bill for $200 and immediately paid it. But when the same bill kept arriving every month, William angrily inquired what was happening. "What?" confessed his brother, "You did tell me to pay it forward for Uncle Charlie! So, I rented him a tuxedo."[41]

---

[41] "Unable to Attend the Funeral," Reddit Post, R/Jokes, August 26, 2020, https://www.reddit.com/r/Jokes/comments/igxjv7/unable_to_attend_the_funeral_after_his_uncle/.

Paying it forward is not a dead practice. In fact, if we are alive in Christ, we are commanded by Scripture to serve the Lord (Psalm 100:2). Because He first loved us, we can "pay it forward" by serving where He calls us to serve. In doing God's work, we serve Him, not the local congregation, not the head deacon or elder, not the preacher or some committee. Our focus should be to serve the Lord. We worship and serve Him alone—not people! Notice that the impetus is neither guilt-ridden nor resenting; we are pressed to serve the Lord "with gladness."

When serving God, it is impossible to serve Him without humbly serving one another (Philippians 2:3–4). When we serve people out of utter happiness, humility, and humanitarian love, we, in turn, serve the Lord in the way He intended. Jesus told His disciples that He did not come to be served but to serve others and that *"The greatest among you will be your servant"* (Mark 10:45; Matthew 23:11 NIV). He then modeled His words during the last supper when He rose from the table, wrapped Himself with a towel, and washed the disciples' dirty feet (John 13:5). Jesus promised that those who served others would be blessed (John 13:15–17). As we love to serve others, the amazing truth is that we will actually be blessed and filled with joy. Perhaps that is why JOY stands for **J**esus first, **O**thers second, and **Y**ou last.

The joy of serving God comes from knowing that we are fulfilling our divine purpose and trusting that our salvation is not dependent upon how well and how often we serve God. Serving our Father is not a requirement to enter Heaven. That notion alone should cause us to make a joyful noise to the Lord. In the original Hebrew, the Psalmist calls for a trumpet like noise and shouting that gushes from people where emotions are uncontained, the type of whooping we hear at a sports arena.

To experience this level of amazing joy, we should serve God not for the applause of man nor for the repayment of those whom we help (Luke 14:14). Instead, we must serve out of the purity of our hearts and the sincerity of our souls without any sense of obligation. God, then, will supernaturally spill into us a radiant joy. Try blessing a family, for instance, by paying for their groceries. Their excitement and joy will become infectious.

Paying it forward is not a one-time service event either. Instead, we are to devote ourselves regularly to good works (Titus 3:14). A lifestyle of service creates a lifetime of joy. If we have breath in our lungs, unlike Uncle Charlie, God has a mission for each of us. It does not interfere with our journey; it *is* our journey. After all, *"faith without works is dead"* (James 2:26 NKJV).

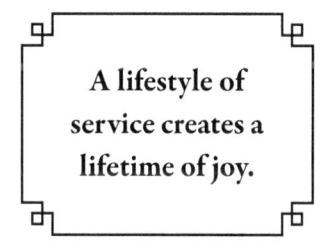

> **A lifestyle of service creates a lifetime of joy.**

Action Challenge: Find a need and fill it. If you see a family in crisis, make them a home-cooked meal. Volunteer your weekend at a local homeless shelter. Develop a relationship with an outcast. Be the hands and feet of Jesus with a willing heart.

_____
_____
_____
_____
_____
_____
_____

Prayer: Dear Lord, help me change my lifestyle to do for others as I would have them do for me. Allow me to see people as You see them. Open my heart to realize their needs, so I might pay it forward and value others more. In Jesus' name, amen.

> *True joy comes when you serve God to get nothing else but more of God.*

Day 23

Joy in Giving

It is more blessed to give than to receive.

(Acts 20:35b KJV)

Two boys were talking about Christmas. One said, "We bought an artificial tree this year."

The other retorted, "Doesn't artificial bother you?"

The first replied, "No, not as long as the presents are real."

This young man may be onto something. A real gift comes from real love. Put differently, it is possible to give without loving, but it is impossible to love without giving. Give to bless, not to impress. Our motives matter far more than our money. Generously giving is not about the size of the gift but the size of the heart.[42]

---

[42] Robert Shannon, and Michael Shannon, Celebrating the Birth of Christ, Cincinnati, Ohio: Standard Publishing, 1985, p. 41.

God loves a cheerful giver (2 Corinthians 9:7). He desires His children to have a lifestyle of giving with a sense of joy in the act of giving rather than a sense of duty or expectation to get something in return. When giving, the Scripture shows how we should not let our "...*left hand know what our right hand is doing*" so that our giving may be done with pure motives (Matthew 6:3 ESV). When we give cheerfully with a pure heart and real love, we will be more blessed to give than to receive (Acts 20:35). Joy is our reward when we give with love. *"For where your treasure is, there your heart will be also"* (Matthew 6:21 NIV).

Why is there such powerful joy in generosity? Neuroscience attempts to answer the question by giving us intricate details about how the dopamine reward pathway is activated when someone donates to a worthy cause. The same way that part of the brain is turned on when we eat a slice of chocolate cake or take a "joy" ride. Scientists may call it the "vibrational energy emitting from one's subconscious," but Christians call it "joy." Biologically, the joy of giving may lead to a happier, healthier life because it triggers chemicals in our brains to improve mood, reduce stress, build cheer, and bring us closer to God.

> **Joy is our reward when we give with love.**

While these justifications are helpful, a much deeper explanation can be found from a biblical view. Giving takes us out of ourselves and permits us to expand beyond our human limitations. When we give cheerfully, we gain insight into how God feels. We begin to see why He is so delighted to give us His love when we participate in His joy by experiencing the satisfaction of blessing others. Consider observing a gift exchange.

Do not watch the recipient; instead, watch the giver. Listen to what he or she says. What we will hear and see is that the one giving the gift will express more joy than the one opening it.

Imagine the jubilee that occurs in Heaven when the free gift of salvation is opened by someone on Earth who finally accepts this glorious salvation gift (Romans 6:23). There is nothing artificial about that present found at the foot of Calvary's tree. On our journey, when we share the gift of eternal life and see it received, be prepared to dance to the joy like what was experienced by the angels (John 3:16; Luke 15:10). It is as real as it gets. Why, then, don't we make it a lifestyle of giving? Everybody can experience the joy and blessing of generosity because everybody has something to give.

Action Challenge: Make a daily habit to give someone a portion of your time, talent, or treasure. Perhaps that means stopping to chat with someone who is alone, giving a handwritten poem to a discouraged friend, or paying for a family's meal at a restaurant without them knowing who paid.

___

Prayer: Thank you, Lord, for showing me what generous giving means. Stir my heart to do the same. I want to give with a cheerful heart when I give of my time, talent, or treasure. Allow joy to be my reward! Prepare the way for me to give the greatest gift of salvation to someone this week. In Jesus' name, amen.

Those who give with joy receive joy as their gift.

Day 24

Joy in Peacemaking

*Deceit is in the hearts of those who plot evil,
but those who promote peace have joy.*

(Proverbs 12:20 NIV)

A man took a trip to the barber, where the stylist asked how his Thanksgiving went. "Oh, it went fine," said the man. "We had a lot of family over, and the wife prepared the meal. I helped out, though. She got a little stressed and told me she needed some peace and quiet in the kitchen so she could finish cooking... so, I removed all the batteries from the smoke detectors."[43]

---

[43] "60 Thanksgiving Jokes to Tell Around The Reunion Table," Little Day Out, January 19, 2022, https://www.littledayout.com/thanksgiving-jokes-to-tell-around-the-reunion-table/.

Sometimes, our batteries run out while keeping relationships going. Anger, bitterness, and conflict steal our joy, leaving no energy to resolve things. However, once the smoke clears, the Bible teaches that the path to restored joy is promoting peace (Proverbs 12:20). The very act of peacemaking springs up joy in our hearts. Why? Because peace is a Fruit of the Spirit, a blessing that God sets free into our lives. Much like any other Fruit of the Spirit, it can only grow to its fullest when we are properly grafted in the Lord. We can never obtain peace in our external relationships until we make peace with ourselves and God first. Simply put, know Jesus... know peace, no Jesus... no peace.

The scriptures describe peace as reconciliation. Paul explains it this way: *"Therefore being justified by faith, we have peace with God through our Lord Jesus Christ"* (Romans 5:1 KJV). Moreover, there is no way to peace; except Jesus is the way to peace. Our ultimate peace has been settled by the Prince of Peace, the Supreme Peacemaker (Isaiah 9:6). That is why Jesus said, *"Blessed are the peacemakers, For they shall be called sons of God"* (Mattew 5:9 NKJV).

Notice how Jesus emphasizes blessed: *Blessed are the peacemakers.* When we make it a lifestyle to promote peace, we are blessed with joy. Christ did not say, "Blessed are the peace wishers," "peace lovers," or "peace hopers." To have joy, peacemakers must confront the troublemakers by sowing seeds of righteousness (James 3:18).

Take, for example, King David, who set out with 400 armed men to slay Nabal and kill every male in his household due to pride. When peacemaker Abigail intervened with fresh food from her kitchen, David praised her with joy saying, *"Blessed be your good sense"* (1 Samual 25:33 NRSV). In a similar vein, when Joseph made peace with his brothers who sold him into slavery, *"the spirit of their father Jacob revived"* (Genesis 45:27 NIV). Joy was restored in Jacob's family. From these examples, it is clear that the battle for peace is worth waging.

Sadly, battles arise out of disputes (Joshua 22:10–34), differences in values and goals (Acts 15:39), competition for resources (Genesis 13:1–2), and sinful habits (James 4:1–2). Peacemaking is a dangerous job because "hurt people hurt people." On our journey to joy, we may have to stand in harm's way or become the target of hostilities from either side. Making peace is not always possible, either (Romans 12:18). Paul recognized the harsh realities of a broken and evil world where reconciliation can fail.

Sometimes, it is best to walk away from a hot kitchen or *"shake the dust off"* and move along (Matthew 10:14 NIV). True peace is not the absence of conflict; it is the presence of joy forged by obedience. God has repeatedly commanded us to reconcile with others by taking the lead to pursue peace rather than waiting for it to arrive—no matter the outcome, joy blooms. To pursue peace requires obedience, humility, and trust in the Lord, qualities that bring joy. Frankly, every bit of Scripture is an approach to promoting peace (2 Corinthians 5:18). Perhaps peacemaking, then, is best explained not as a utensil but as the whole kitchen!

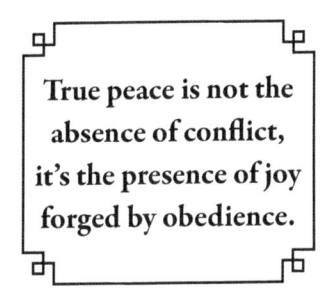

> **True peace is not the absence of conflict, it's the presence of joy forged by obedience.**

Action Challenge: Reconcile a relationship to bring peace today. Start with a gentle answer (Proverbs 15:1). Stop talking badly about others so they can be at peace with you (Psalm 16:7).

Prayer: Oh Lord, give me the courage to bear truth in love so there can be peace and joy. Make me right with You before I make it right with others. In Jesus' name, amen.

Peace is heart-work, which pumps out joy.

Day 25

Joy in Fruit

But the fruit of the Spirit is … joy…

(Galatians 5:22 NIV)

An elderly gentleman living in New Jersey wanted to plant his annual tomato garden, but without help, he would have to let the weeds take over. He wrote to his only son who was in prison, describing his predicament, "Dear Vincent, I am feeling pretty sad because I won't be able to plant my juicy tomato garden this year. I'm getting too old to be digging up the garden plot. If you were here, I know that my troubles would be over because you'd be happy to dig up the plot like the good ole days. Love, Papa."

A few days later, he received a letter from his son asking him not to dig up the garden because that's where all the bodies were buried. At 4 a.m. the next morning, FBI agents and police began digging up the entire area without finding any bodies. They left apologetically. Later that day, the old man received another letter from his son, "Dear Papa, go ahead and plant the tomatoes now. That's the best I could do under the circumstances. Love Vinnie."[44]

---

[44] Gerard Assey, Christian Jokes for the 'Serious Religious' Folks!: A Preachers & Christian

To bear juicy fruit, we must prepare the soil for deep roots. A farmer will not grow fruit by focusing on the fruits. Fruit naturally happens when roots are deep and healthy. The same is true in our spiritual lives when deeply seated roots are filled with the Spirit (Romans 8:9). Only those who are saved from sin can receive the Spirit and experience divine joy. Throughout Scripture, joy and the Spirit are mysteriously linked (Luke 10:21; Romans 14:17; 1 Thessalonians 1:6). In Acts 13:52, when the disciples were filled with the Spirit, they were filled with joy.

Sadly, some people seek joy without the Spirit. They only produce groves of artificial fruit that often get passed off as Fruit of the Spirit, yet it is nothing more than fake fruit painted over with gloss that fades in the elements. When the winds blow, their fruit withers and dies because they have no roots in Christ. It is one thing to have joy when everything is going well. It is another thing altogether to maintain our joy when the bottom falls out.

Authentic believers, however, make a lifestyle of connecting their roots to the True Vine, becoming branches full of His joy and vitality (John 15:5). One of the nine fruits of the Spirit is *joy*. Only the Spirit can produce joyful fruit in us (Galatians 5:22). It is the Fruit of the Spirit that's the outward expression of God's nature within us. The more we embrace His love and promises, spiritual fruit will appear naturally in our lives, and the more we will become *"filled with an inexpressible and glorious joy,"* no matter how the wind blows (1 Peter 1:8). True believers do not show the Fruit of the Spirit to be saved; we grow fruit because we have been saved.

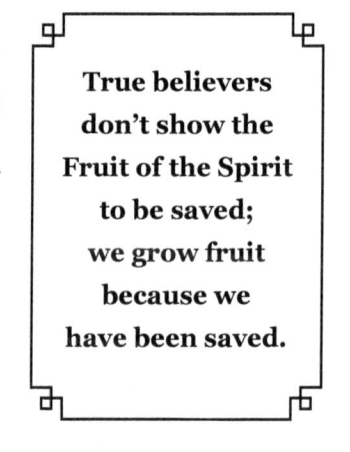

> True believers don't show the Fruit of the Spirit to be saved; we grow fruit because we have been saved.

Ministers' Companion, (Independently published, 2020), Section 162.

While the growth of fruit begins with a seed, the day the seed is planted is not the day the fruit is picked. Fruit may be considered fast food, but it does not grow fast. On our journey to joy, we will see that the last thing to grow on a tree is the fruit. It takes a lifestyle and a lifetime of fertilizing with the Word of God and dousing with the Water of life (John 4:14) to bear fruit that is ripe, juicy, and sweet in His perfect time. In time, more fruit will grow to produce other fruit. Yes, we may know how many seeds are in a tomato, yet only God knows how many tomatoes are in a seed.

No one may know how many tomatoes Papa grew in his garden, but we do know hundreds of seeds were ready to be sown. We might not need the FBI to do our dirty work, yet we do need the grace of God in us to nurture the right fruit. After all, *a tree is known by its fruit* (Matthew 12:33). When our heart is a garden, our obedience is the seeds. We can grow joy, or we can grow weeds.

Action Challenge: Instead of looking at yourself, take ten looks at Jesus, saying, "In Christ, I am… fruitful, free, new, chosen, adopted, precious, blessed, able, appointed, and His." As you drive your roots deeper into those truths, fruit will naturally blossom.

_____
_____
_____
_____
_____
_____
_____
_____

Prayer: O God, thank you for planting my seed in the rich soil cultivated by the Holy Spirit so that my deep roots can grow fresh fruit. Prune and protect me from the wild elements. In Jesus' name, amen.

God prefers the fruits of joy over religious nuts.

Day 26

Joy in Prayer

Ask and you will receive, and your joy will be complete.

(John 16:24b NIV)

A teacher's little six-year-old girl had been so naughty during the week that her mother decided to give her the worst kind of punishment. She told her she could not go to the school picnic on Saturday. When the day came, her mother felt she had been too harsh and changed her mind. When she told the little girl she could go to the picnic, the child's reaction was one of doom and gloom. So, her mom, thinking that she would be excited to go to the picnic, asked her daughter what the problem was. "It's too late!" the little girl said. "I've already prayed for rain!"[45]

---

[45] "Didn't See That Coming," The Cybersalt Site, Accessed January 29, 2024, https://www.cybersalt.org/clean-jokes/didnt-see-that-coming.

It has been said, "If you only pray when you're in trouble, you're in trouble."

While running late, troubled Fred needed to park fast. So, he prayed, "God, I beg for pity. If You find a spot, I'll give up drugs, drinking, and dice." Miraculously, a parking spot opened. Fred looked up saying, "Never mind, I found one!" In plots like these, it becomes obvious why our prayer life becomes dull and boring. However, a lifestyle of prayer doesn't have to be that way.[46]

When we find fellowship with Jesus, prayer becomes the world's greatest wireless connection to the storehouses of God's infinite joy. Prayer also becomes the key that unlocks those storehouses. As prayers get answered, we get joy. Jesus taught that if we simply ask, we will receive, and our joy will be full (John 16:24). And yet, we have not because we ask not (James 4:3). "The great tragedy of life is not unanswered prayer, but unoffered prayer."[47] If we make no time for prayer, we make no parking spot in our hearts for joy.

While answered prayer gives us joy on our spiritual journey, so does the act of prayer. We must come to Him with a pure, teachable, and innocent heart that strays away from meaningless repetition or empty words (Matthew 6:7). He is more interested in our hearts than our hubbub. When we pray, it is better to have a heart without words than words without a heart.

---

[46] "Humor," Ofthisandthat, Accessed January 29, 2024, https://ofthisandthat.org/Humor.html.

[47] "Quote by K. B. Meyer," Famous Quotes & Authors, 2011, https://www.famousquotesandauthors.com/authors/kb__meyer_quotes.html.

Once the condition of our heart is ready, prayer becomes the speedway to the source of joy. The Bible's roadmap offers countless routes to get there. By heading straight on Tribute Street, we either praise God out of joy or receive joy out of praising God (Psalm 30:4). If we take a U-turn onto Confession Road, we receive joy by reversing course from sin and removing our guilt (Psalm 51:7–8). By making a right turn on Gratitude Highway, we encounter joy because thankful prayer lifts us from circumstances to remind us of His many blessings (1 Thessalonians 3:9). When strolling down Petition Lane, we breathe in fresh joy by simply asking for healing, courage, wisdom, and so on (Jeremiah 33:3; James 1:5).

On our path, we can either let prayer become our steering wheel or spare tire. He can either be in control of our lives or out of our lives. When we have no faith to pray, we miss the joy of His presence and presents. Additionally, we do not have to miss the aspects of prayer that bring showers of joy, perhaps because there is a little child out there praying on our behalf for rain. Of all the onramps to joy, prayer is the quickest path to God's joy. He receives joy when we pray, then pours it right back to us tenfold. Imagine, though, if we made a lifestyle of constant prayer, we would have a lifetime of overflowing joy direct from the source (1 Thessalonians 5:16). It starts with childlike faith, humbly taking God at His Word (Mark 10:14). As children innocently trust their earthly fathers, we should trust our Heavenly Father who *"...gives good gifts to those who ask him,"* no matter how small the request (Matthew 7:11 NIV). If prayer becomes a habit, then joy becomes a lifestyle.

Action Challenge: Each morning, pray genuine words like, "Lord, please sanctify my heart, head, and hands today. Give me peace of heart, clarity of mind, strength of hands to glorify You."

_____
_____
_____
_____
_____
_____
_____

Prayer: Oh God, strengthen my prayer life. Help me to pray as I can, not as I cannot. Nudge me to pray when I am doing mindless tasks. Prompt me to lift the needs of others. In Jesus' name, amen.

We can't get deep into joy until we get deep into prayer.

Day 27

Joy in Advising

A person finds joy in giving an apt reply—

(Proverbs 15:23 NIV)

Joe set up his friend Michael to go on a blind date with a friend of a friend of his. He advised Michael that all would work out okay. Hesitantly, Michael then asked, "What do I do if she's ugly? I'll be stuck with her all night." Joe then encouraged him not to worry that if he didn't like what he saw that he should just shout, "Aaaaauuuggghhh!" By faking an asthma attack, he would have a sure exit plan. That night, Mike knocked on Jill's door. When she came out, he was awe-struck at her beauty. Just as he was about to speak, the young lady suddenly shouted, "Aaaaauuuggghhh!"[48]

---

[48] "Joke: Blind Date," JokeBarn.com, August 25, 1999, https://www.jokebarn.com/388/blind-date/.

Words matter (James 3:9). They are like berries; the wrong kind can prove lethal. Advice can bring harm or harmony. Words can give life or break someone's spirit (Proverbs 15:4). They can subdue anger or stir it up (Proverbs 15:1). And yet, gracious words are sweet to the soul and healing to the bones when speaking the truth in love--tender without surrender (Proverbs 16:24; Ephesians 4:15). Saying the right thing, in the right way, at just the right time creates joy (Proverbs 15:23).

As Christians, we have a duty to use a wise tongue. And yet, how do we receive wisdom to offer good counsel that results in righteous joy? It begins with fearing (respecting) the Lord as Isaiah did (Proverbs 9:10; Isaiah 50:4).

> **Saying the right thing
> – in the right way
> – at just the right time
> creates joy.**

Once humble, we can have *"wisdom from above"* (James 3:17 ESV). Wisdom comes not from horoscopes or the stars but from the Son who made those stars (1 John 3:7). It comes from keeping company with wise believers (Proverbs 13:20). We cannot soar with the eagles if we are running with the turkeys.

We also receive wisdom by asking for it (James 1:5) and through careful examination of Scripture, the source of wisdom. This preparation helps us ensure our answers to those whom we are advising are correct (Proverbs 15:28). A lifestyle of studying the Bible will equip us with certain words of *truth* rather than mere opinions (Proverbs 22:17-22; 1 Peter 3:15). Accordingly, wisdom will lead us *"...to a life of joy and peace"* (Proverbs 3:17 ERV).

Joy stems from wisdom oozes out when giving an apt reply. A timely word is delightful--both to the giver and receiver. Whether this is a word of correction, criticism, countering, comfort, or coaching, "in righteousness--the best word to speak is one that is in agreement with God's Word on the matter."[49] When Truth is not the foundation, advice remains rightfully necessary but not necessarily right.

For advice to be right, we must also think before we speak and pray before we think. Throughout Scripture, this pattern is modeled. Joshua spoke the perfect word to correct Israel from journeying down the wrong paths. David spoke the perfect word to criticize Goliath for mocking God. Daniel had the perfect words to clarify Nebuchadnezzar's dream. Jesus always had the perfect word to counter detractors, comfort those who were needy, and coach His disciples in righteousness. Each of these biblical characters experienced joy when they offered their sage advice.

Whether we are positioned to advise a friend for a blind date or the aftermath of a blind date, we should be ready with an apt reply. Yes, it may be enticing to fake an asthma attack and run the other way, but God has called us to rise up and advise *"for such as time as this"* (Esther 4:14 NIV). May we allow our measured speech to be timely seasoned with grace and wisdom so that joy springs up (1 Peter 3:10), no matter how ugly the situation might be, lest we feel compelled to shout, " AAAAAUUUGGGHHH!"

---

[49] J. Palmer, "Joy By The Answer of the Mouth," Living Water Ministries (blog), October 22, 2020, https://livingwaterministries.blog/2020/10/22/joy-by-the-answer-of-the-mouth/.

Action Challenge: Listen to the lyrics from *Speak Life* by Toby Mac. In every encounter today, make a conscious effort to bring others joy by giving an apt reply filled with hope and encouragement.

_____
_____
_____
_____
_____
_____
_____

Prayer: Holy Father, thank you for sending Your Son to be my Shepherd. Help me hear His voice through Your Word and the wise counsel of spiritual friends. In Jesus' name, amen.

A true, timely word fills life with joy when true to the timeless Word.

Day 28

Joy in Soul-Winning

Indeed, [converts] you are our glory and joy.

(1 Thessalonians 2:20 NIV)

A barber felt led to share his faith more with his customers. So, he decided when he awoke the next morning, he would witness to the first man who walked through his door. Soon after opening the shop, the first customer came in asking for a shave. The barber obliged, saying, "Sure, just sit here, and I'll be with you in a moment." Meanwhile, the barber went in the back room to pray a quick, desperate prayer, "Oh God, give me the wisdom to know just the right thing to say to my first customer today. Amen." Then, unwittingly, the barber came out with his razor knife in one hand and a Bible in the other while saying, "Good morning, sir. I have but one question for you... are you ready to die?"[50]

---

[50] "The Christian Barber," ChristiansUnite.com, 2019, https://jokes.christiansunite.com/Bible/The_Christian_Barber.shtml.

Soul-winning is a biblical term that should not be scary for either the lost soul or the soul-winner, yet we should be wise in how we evangelize (Proverbs 11:30). We do not stand in the world bearing witness to Jesus. Instead, we stand in Jesus, bearing witness to the world. Scripture shows that soul-winning is more about being than being perfect. It is not about an ability that God is looking for in us, but usability. When our capabilities are of God, we are never incapable of winning souls. It is the chief business of every true believer to *"go and make disciples of all nations"* (Matthew 28:19 NIV). When two-thirds of God's name is **go**, we realize how important soul-winning is. Jesus demonstrated this as His final act by winning a thief to Himself (Luke 23:43).

Soul-winning may be an obligation and a commandment to fulfill, but its fruit gushes with a fulfillment of joy. Soul-winning brings joy to God and the angels when one sinner repents (Luke 15:10). All of Heaven rejoices when the lost are found. Heaven is eager with excitement when believers seek out lost souls!

> **We do not stand in the world bearing witness to Jesus; instead, we stand in Jesus bearing witness to the world.**

Soul-winning brings joy not only in Heaven but also great joy on Earth. When the Ethiopian Eunuch realized the value of his soul and was converted, he *"went on his way rejoicing"* (Acts 8:39 NIV). He found joy after learning God's truth. He found joy after being transformed and freed from sin's guilt. He found joy from his new hope for eternal life. All of these discoveries converged together into an unrivaled rejoicing.

Soul-winners and fellow Christians also experience great joy on Earth when sinners find faith in God. Because faith comes through hearing, we must use both *testament* and *testimony* while sharing the Good News (Romans 10:17). Then again, the gospel is only good news if it gets there in time. Most unsaved in the world are not unreachable--simply unreached. That is why Paul and Barnabas wasted no time on their soul-winning journey. They reported the conversion of many Gentiles from their hard work, as it *"brought great joy to all the brothers"* (Acts 15:3 ESV). Everyone rejoiced *"with songs of joy"* because the soul-winners could not remain quiet; thus, their seeds bore fruit (Psalm 126:6 NIV).

It has been said that barbers also cannot stay quiet while cutting people's hair. If we believe in Christ, we cannot stay silent either! When life and death are balanced on a razor, we must make a lifestyle of sowing seeds, allowing others to water, and trusting our God of wisdom to give the increase (1 Corinthians 3:6). When we do shave our fear and lead someone to Christ, no greater joy will be experienced and celebrated both in Heaven and on Earth.

Action Challenge: List two or three people you encounter who may not have a relationship with Jesus. Next to each name, write a time and location that you plan to share your testimony with each of them this week. Pray for these individuals before sharing.

_____

_____

_____

_____

_____

_____

_____

Prayer: O Lord, I pray that You would open doors for me to share the gospel with boldness, clarity, and gentleness. Move in ways I have never seen before and draw unbelievers to You so that they might be transformed by Your saving grace. In Jesus' name, amen.

> *Making disciples of Jesus is the overflow of the JOY in being disciples of Jesus.*

Day 29

Joy in Praise

Praise God with shouts of joy, all people!

(Psalm 66:1 GNT)

A cocky guy named Bill decided to check out the truth behind an ad he saw for a Christian horse. The horse's owner explained the ease in riding him by making him go with the words, "Praise the Lord!" and forcing him to stop with the word "Amen!" Bill smugly got onto the horse, shouting, "Praise the Lord!" Sure enough, the horse started to walk. "Praise the Lord!" he said again, and the horse trotted. "Praise the Lord! Praise the Lord!" he yelled, and the horse galloped. Bossy Bill enjoyed his ride so much that he nearly overlooked the cliff they were about to go over. Frantically, he belted, "AMEN!" The horse came to a screeching halt at the cliff's edge. Overcome with relief, Bill said, "Phew! Praise the Lord!"[51]

---

[51] "Let Everything That Has Breath Praise the Lord! | Sermon Joke by Dr. Madana Kumar," Faith Lutheran Church, Accessed January 29, 2024, https://www.faithlutheranchurch.org/sermons/let-everything-has-breath-praise-lord.

The path labeled "Pride" will lead anyone over a cliff (Proverbs 16:18). Such arrogance is hazardous to our well-being because it keeps us from fearing the Lord (Proverbs 22:4). By contrast, humility is the foundation of genuinely praising Him because He is all good. Praise, then, is the portal to divine joy, giving us a foretaste of Heaven. It is the man's natural response to the supernatural presence of Yahweh. Glorifying Him brings us joy, and that joy bursts out of us in the form of praise. We cannot have joy without praise, and it is impossible to praise without feeling joy.

God is not valued at all unless He is valued above all. When we aim to grasp God's goodness and credit to Him all the honor that is due Him through praise, we worry less. Because the goodness of God is unrelenting towards us by His enduring love, He is indeed worthy of praise and inhabits our praise (Psalm 118:1, 22:3). In the moments we take our eyes off ourselves and place them on the goodness of the Lord, we experience joy. Joy comes when we say, "O God, You are good even when life doesn't feel so good."

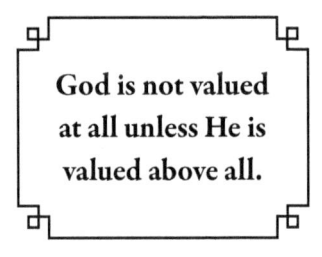

> **God is not valued at all unless He is valued above all.**

Let us journey back in time to the land of Judah, where God's goodness led to praise. King Jehoshaphat learned of three armies marching towards them. Terrified, he fasted and prayed (2 Chronicles 20:2, 12). Then God assured them to stand firm and be unafraid during His deliverance. Judah's men bowed down, praising God with loud voices. Rather than forging their weapons, they put their praise and worship team in front of the army and marched to the battlefield led by singers who sang of His goodness, giving *"thanks to the LORD, for his love endures forever"* (2 Chronicles 20:21 NIV).

True to His promise, God forced the three enemy armies to attack and destroy each other. Judah's praise team shot not one arrow nor maneuvered one horse. They just watched in awe of what the Lord did, collected their spoil, and praised God in the Valley of Berakah (meaning "praise"). Then, the men returned *"joyfully to Jerusalem,"* where they celebrated in the temple with harps, lyres, and trumpets (2 Chronicles 20:27 NIV) Their war cry was praise!

If God can crush three armies all by the courts of praise, He can deliver us from our toughest cliffhangers by simply praising Him. We are called to praise God with shouts of joy, much like the people of Judah (Psalm 66:1). We cannot just belt out "praise the Lord" and expect Him to gallop to our command. Instead, we must humbly come to a screeching halt to what we are doing and make a lifestyle of praising God for His goodness in all things. After all, the ultimate test of joy is not how loudly we praise the Lord in happy times but how deeply we trust Him in dark times.

Action Challenge: Take a moment to name three things you can praise God for today as you reflect on His goodness. Out of genuine humility and gratitude, shout out your praise accompanied by a song like *House of The Lord* by Phil Wickham.

___

___

___

___

___

___

___

Prayer: Loving God, even during hard times, stir in my heart and on my lips the rich spirit of joyful praise to You. May You receive all the glory, honor, and praise due to Your name today as I surrender myself to Your purpose alone. In Jesus' name, amen.

> *Do not let life affect your joyful praise;*
> *let your joyful praise effect life.*

Day 30

Joy in Singing

Come, let us sing joy to the LORD.

(Psalm 95:1a NIV)

Abi was asked by a funeral director to sing at a graveside service for a homeless man who had no family or friends. The program was to be held at a Pauper's Cemetery, out in the country, with a weak cellular and navigation signal. Not familiar with the area, Abigail got lost. Because she arrived an hour late, only the digging crew was left, and they were off eating lunch. She decided to walk up to the gravesite to begin singing Amazing Grace.

With such great emotion, Abi drew in the workers who huddled around to sing and weep with her. After praying a benediction, Abi headed for her car with her head hung low but her heart full of joy. Just as she began to open her car door, she overheard a gravedigger say, "I've never seen nothin' like that before, and I've been putting in septic tanks for twenty years."[52]

---

[52] Dano Janowski, Rabbit And Cat's Pandemic Jokes #7 For Such A Time As This: Even In Pandemics You Gotta Laugh, (Rabbit & Cat Comics, 2020).

Hope is never lost more than we are. However, when we are lost on our journey, "we know with confident hope that we will join our Bride Groom in glory singing a new song before the throne"[53] (Revelation 5:9, 14:3). Through singing, we can find peace to our past, joy to our present, and hope to our future (Psalm 5:11; Proverbs 23:18). We must never fear an unknown future to a known God. Colossians 3 brings this out simply but impressively, directing us to sing "to God" because He is the object of our praise. Ephesians 5:19b (NIV) says, "Sing and make music from your heart to the Lord." It is to Him and about Him that we sing! "Singing has such a unique way of bringing our heart, soul, mind, and strength together to focus entirely and completely on God."[54] In an era of distraction, singing demands the attention of all our senses to focus on Him.

When we sing, we walk a God-designed pathway *in* joy, not *to* joy. After all, joy is a journey, not a destination. On this journey, music touches our emotions in such a way that we are literally able to sense our communication with God; it brings joy to our souls. When there is music in our soul, there is soul in our music.

> **When we make a habit of singing, the presence of God inhabits our praise.**

The Israelites had soul in their music when they dedicated Solomon's Temple. *"...Four thousand were praising the Lord with the instruments which David made for giving praise"* (1 Chronicles 23:5 NASB). Imagine worshipping with 4,000 voices and instruments while singing to God! Their music was thunder and joy, filled with lightning bolts of happiness and praise, foot-stomping, dance-shouting, and cheer-clapping soul singing. The praises were so great that a cloud entered the Temple, flooding the

---

53   Stephen Unthank, "Music in Worship: Sing with Joy," 2018, https://www.placefortruth.org/blog/music-worship-sing-joy.
54   "Nghiep Gia Hoang, St. Anthony Church, Weiner," Catholic Diocese of Little Rock, 2023, https://www.dolr.org/clergy/nghiep-gia-hoang.

place to the point that the priests could not see what they were doing. That cloud was the visible presence of the glory of God.

When we make a habit of singing, the presence of God inhabits our praise (Psalm 22:3). A lifestyle of singing will thus give us a lifetime of joy. We do not sing because we are joyful; we are joyful because we sing. And yet, those who do not sing may be digging their grave even deeper. God is worthy of our praise. Without a song, life would be a sad tune. Music gives us a language to express what words cannot. Too many skeletons in the closet? Too sad to sing? Cannot sing? Sing anyway. God tells us to *"make a joyful noise,"* not a perfect note (Psalm 100:1 ESV). To Him, it is all harmonized.

So, let us make a joyful noise up to the ultimate homeland of music, even if we get lost in the lyrics or our noise sounds like a funeral dirge. Practice makes perfect as we sing to prepare for Heaven. Since singing to God produces joy, "nobody dreams of music in Hell, and nobody conceives of Heaven without it."[55]

---

[55] "Quote by S. Parkes Cadman," Quotefancy, 2024, https://quotefancy.com/quote/1626882/S-Parkes-Cadman-Nobody-dreams-of-music-in-hell-and-nobody-conceives-of-heaven-without-it.

Action Challenge: What music will your life express for God today? Sing along with Kari Jobe and Cody Carnes as though you're summoning the heavens. Scan this QR code for *The Blessing*.

_____
_____
_____
_____
_____
_____
_____
_____

Prayer: Heavenly Father, You create the melodies and harmonies of our lives. You welcome us to move in rhythm with You. "May the song of our hearts be overflowing with joy and may the tune of our lives be pure and true. In Jesus' name, amen."[56]

Singing is the universal language of joy.

---

[56] Laurie Zuverink, "Joy in Worship," Today Daily Devotional: Reframe Ministries, 2018, https://todaydevotional.com/devotions/joy-in-worship /.

Day 31

Joy in Fellowship

Then make my joy complete by being like-minded...

(Philippians 2:2 NIV)

A man flew south to Florida, checked into a hotel, and sent an arrival email to his wife from a lobby computer. By mistake, he sent the email to a widow who just returned from her husband's funeral. While opening Outlook and expecting condolence notes, she fainted after reading, "To my loving wife, I know you're surprised to hear from me; they have computers down here, and we can send emails to loved ones. I've just checked in. How are you and the kids? The place is hotter than I expected, and I'm very lonely here. So, I've made the necessary arrangements for your arrival tomorrow. Expecting you, darling. I can't wait to see you."[57]

---

[57] "Her Husband Typed His Wife's Email Wrong. The Result? So Bad It's Funny!!!," Littlethings, 2014, https://littlethings.com/lifestyle/wrong-email/293635-1.

"Hell is no one but yourself, forever and ever,"[58] quoted C. S. Lewis. Whether or not Hell is a lonely place is anyone's guess, but here on Earth, loneliness may feel like Hell. Yes, we can feel lonely in a crowd. "Being lonely does not mean you are lonely, and being lonely does not mean you are alone."[59] Loneliness is part of the journey of life and is proof that we have an innate desire for connection.

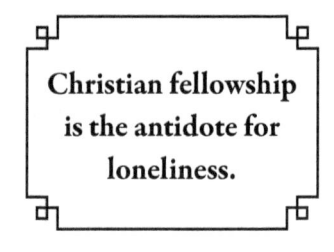

> **Christian fellowship is the antidote for loneliness.**

Christian fellowship is the antidote for loneliness. God created us for fellowship, which so happens to produce joy. Just as in the beginning, God sought fellowship with Adam, and He lovingly seeks fellowship with us today. Since the Holy Trinity is within Himself a fellowship and source of joy, image-bearing believers will find fullness of joy by having a lifestyle of fellowship with God (2 Corinthians 13:14). Sadly, many Christians do not have fellowship with God; they have fellowship with each other about God. And yet, both are key.

Just as God called us to fellowship with Him (1 Corinthians 1:9), we must fellowship with like-minded believers (1 John 1:3). Be careful not to confuse socializing with fellowship. Socializing shares earthly life, like joining a Florida beach party. Christian fellowship, though, shares spiritual life like joining those who practice hospitality or encouragement (Romans 12:13; Hebrews 10:25). Jesus and John say this gospel-focused fellowship brings *complete unity* and *complete joy* (John 17:21; 2 John 1:12). Heavenly joy cannot be obtained by worldly influence, nor does it come from being apart from other believers. The Christian who regularly is in the company of fellow

---

[58] "Quote by C. S. Lewis." "Are People in Hell Isolated and Alone?" | Probe Ministries (blog), September 27, 2001, https://probe.org/are-people-in-hell-isolated-and-alone/.

[59] "Quote by John Spence," Quotefancy, 2024, https://quotefancy.com/quote/1698001/John-Spence-Being-alone-does-not-mean-you-are-lonely-and-being-lonely-does-not-mean-you.

saints, fulfilling the characteristics of fellowship, will invariably experience divine joy. Who we surround ourselves with shape who we are.

Association promotes assimilation. If we surround ourselves with toxic people, we will become toxic people. When we surround ourselves with joyful people, we will become joyful people. All of us need fellowship to be a place of grace, where mistakes are not rubbed in but rubbed out. Some talk to us in their free time, while some free their time to talk to us. Much like crossed emails, we must be careful not to send mixed signals. Translation: free our time for others to develop a deep, eternal relationship with one another. After all, it is a foretaste of life in Heaven.

Before God makes the necessary arrangements for our heavenly arrival, what are we doing now to have fellowship with Him and like-minded Christians? Do we bring joy to other believers when they think of us, much like the joy brought to Paul when he thought of his friends? He also grieved over those who did not know Jesus for one day they would arrive at a place much hotter and lonelier, apart from God (Romans 6:23; 2 Thessalonians 1:9). What are we doing to prevent people from checking in to the wrong eternal residence? Invite them to a Godly fellowship where those who live in the Lord never see each other for the last time.

Action Challenge: If you are a member of a small group, make a group covenant that includes characteristics of biblical fellowship: authenticity, encouragement, sympathy, forgiveness, honesty, humility, courtesy, confidentiality, and frequency.

_____
_____
_____
_____
_____
_____
_____

Prayer: Lord, I acknowledge my need for others. I ask You to lead me to relationships that will bring joy to the Church because of our unity, humility, and unselfishness. In Jesus' name, amen.

> *The next best thing to being joyful, is for one to live in a circle of those who are.*

Day 32

Joy in Celebrating

Rejoice in the Lord always; again I will say rejoice.

(Philippians 4:4 ESV)

When a young monk arrived at a monastery, he was tasked to hand copy the old laws of the Church. Alarmed that he was to copy from replicas, he complained to the head monk that just one error could get passed down to subsequent copies. The head monk, conceding the bind, tiptoed down beneath the monastery where the original manuscripts were vaulted. Hours went by with no sighting of the head monk, so the young monk rushed to the catacombs only to witness the elder banging his head against the wall and wailing, "We missed the R! We missed the R! We missed the R!" Then he followed up with, "The word is... celebrate!"[60]

---

60 Lucy Blackman, Have You Heard the One About... Religion, (Bloomington: iUniverse Publishing, 2011), p. 39.

Words matter, but so do our actions. Just as we are called to weep with those who weep, we are instructed to celebrate with those who celebrate (Romans 12:15). It is the Times Square for all the other spiritual disciplines on this journey. Without a joyful spirit of festivity, the disciplines become dreary vehicles for mindless travels. God never intended for Christians to live dry, boring lives, which is why we see celebrations both commanded and practiced throughout Scripture. Jesus, for example, came so that we can have abundant life, including celebration (John 10:10).

> **Without a joyful spirit of festivity, the disciplines become dreary vehicles for mindless travels.**

No one wishes to celebrate the good news of a victory or event all alone. Our first tendency is to call someone to share the joy of the good news. In our excitement, we may want to bring out the best turkey, the best tableware, and the best tunes to *"...have a feast and celebrate"* (Luke 15:23 NIV). Jesus did this by turning water into wine to prolong the joy for a wedding party (John 2:1-11). From this, we learn that people celebrate because they are overjoyed, yet they can become overjoyed because they celebrate.

We need each other to practice a lifestyle of celebration and to experience contagious joy in every season (Philippians 4:4; Proverbs 15:13). However, we must never overshadow *how* we celebrate and with *whom* we celebrate. Celebrating victories and completed projects is great (Nehemiah 12), yet we must celebrate unto the Lord (Exodus 12:14). We may revel in our good news, but how about the Good News of Jesus? His joyful story is found in the name of the special day when we celebrate Christ's birth.

If we travel back across the sands of time to the first Christmas, we see Mary excitedly visiting with cousin Elizabeth to announce her pregnancy. Out of hearing the good news, John the Baptist leaped in his mother's womb (Luke 1:41). The angel also brought good tidings of great joy to the shepherds who accepted this celebration and visited the Good News in a manger (Luke 2:10).

Today, we do not set out to visit Jesus in a manger, but we do set out replica manger scenes. Over 25% of Americans celebrate Christmas by putting up decorations before Thanksgiving.[61] They desire to stretch the experience of contagious joy. In a culture of stress and strain, the ambiance of Christmas lifts our spirits and comforts our hearts. We do not have to rush to the catacombs to find the truth about joy. The word is... celebrate! True joy and celebration come from a right relationship with God (Psalm 1:1). We do not have to bang our heads to learn that celebrations are more fun when shared, especially as the Lord is merrily celebrated.

May we not let Christmas be the only day to celebrate Jesus. Instead, may we make it a disciplined lifestyle of daily celebrating the joy of our salvation (Psalm 51:12). When we do, the heart of celebration must be a celebration from the heart.

---

61   Sarah Gambles, "Do You Put up Christmas Decorations before or after Thanksgiving?" Yahoo News, November 26, 2023, https://news.yahoo.com/put-christmas-decorations-thanksgiving-052017418.html.

Action Challenge: Practice in the joyful celebration of others today (i.e., promotions, graduations, and births). Then, celebrate God's miracles in your life (i.e., healings, bonuses, and baptisms).

_____

_____

_____

_____

_____

_____

_____

Prayer: Lord, I celebrate how prophecy was fulfilled in Your birth, burial, and resurrection. I adore You, not just on Christmas day, but every day. Oh, Jesus, I dance with joy in my heart. In Jesus' name, amen.

Joy on earth will come to stay when we celebrate Christmas every day.

Day 33

Joy in Labor

...rejoice in labor––this is the gift of God.

(Ecclesiastes 5:19 NKJV)

A handyman knocked on neighborhood doors for work when he met an old man in his backyard garage. After giving his spiel about mowing lawns, fixing fences, or power washing windows, the handyman sold the senior citizen on painting the porch in the front. Due to its size, the man in the garage figured it would take all day to paint that huge porch. Then, two hours later, the young man came sweeping through the shop to share the news that he had completed the job. Perplexed by how fast the big porch was painted, the elderly neighbor asked how that was possible. "Aw, it ain't that big. And besides, it ain't a Porsche; it's a BMW!"[62]

---

62 "A Guy Looking for Work," Jokes by Scout Life, May 27, 2007, https://jokes.scoutlife.org/jokes/a-guy-looking-for-work/.

Anyone can do bad work, but not everyone does good work. Even if we are never recognized on Earth for our honest labor, we can feel joy knowing one day we will get a *reward from the Lord* or hear Him say, *"Well done"* (Colossians 3:23-24; Matthew 25:23). Our work matters greatly to God, especially when we glorify Him by faithfully aligning our God-given gifts and talents with His call while centered within His perfect will. Our efforts become beautifully painted billboards along the journey for His Kingdom. By faithfully laboring, we emulate the Almighty's creativity, order, and delight for beauty and excellence.

When God fashioned the universe, He delighted in work (Genesis 1:31), called His work *"good"* (Genesis 2:2), and found joy in it (Philippians 2:13). Work, then, did not result from sin; but from creation as a gift for us to enjoy the fruits of our labor. While filled with

> While filled with fruit and honey, paradise was not a vacation. It was a vocation.

fruit and honey, *paradise* was not a vacation. It was a vocation. Work was so important that Scripture mentions it over 800 times in many forms, more than all words used to express worship, music, praise, and singing combined. Aptly arranged, the Hebrew word *avodah* for "work" also means "worship" or "work-ship."[63] Adonai creatively designed our work and worship to become a seamless lifestyle of living so that we can experience a lifetime of joy.

No matter the setting, when we live a lifestyle of "work-ship," we glorify God, and He gladdens us with joy. Sadly, today, many view work as a burden, not as a blessing. Jerome K. Jerome quips, "I like work ... I can sit and look at it for hours."[64]

---

[63] Austin Burkhart, "Avodah: A Seamless Life of Work, Worship, and Service," Institute for Faith, Work & Economics, March 31, 2015, https://tifwe.org/avodah-a-life-of-work-worship-and-service/.

[64] "Quote by Jerome K. Jerome," Goodreads, Inc., 2024, https://www.goodreads.com/quotes/1407-i-like-work-it-fascinates-me-i-can-sit-and.

Humor aside, work is not intended to be attended but to be accomplished. In turn, accomplishment grows our joy. As image bearers, our labor has intrinsic value where we reflect the identity of our Creator. Just as He receives joy in work, so can we gain joy (Ecclesiastes 3:13, 5:19).

Our work *"in the Lord"* is never in vain (1 Corinthians 15:58 NIV). Although, when our identity conversely becomes more in work than in Christ, our joy wanes. While work can give us meaning in life, we must be careful not to make work the meaning of life. Even the most faithful believers can become so engrossed in the work of the Lord that they forget the Lord of the work. Instead, God desires—whether painting porches, restoring BMWs, etc. —that every work we pursue to be a *"work of faith"* (2 Thessalonians 1:11). The work we are given is to be labored for His sake and to be done with meaningful strength and joy that He supplies (1 Peter 4:11).

When we journey in joy, work will not give us meaning until we find meaning in the Lord who gave us work. That meaning, that purpose gives our work life, which then stirs our work to give us life. A life of joy begins *"to him who knocks"* and invites God into "work-ship" (Matthew 7:8 NKJV). Doing so opens the door to our hearts so that we can recognize that the privilege to work is a gift, the passion to work is a blessing, and the pleasure of work is success.

Action Challenge: Which adage fits you: "I live to work" or "I work to live"? After reading Genesis chapters 1 and 2, describe how you can connect with God's work to find internal meaning and live to work.

___

___

___

___

___

___

___

Prayer: Almighty, may all of our work as image bearers be a common grace given to believers and unbelievers alike. Thank You for the joy of serving in this way. In Jesus' name, amen.

Joy comes in our work when Christ works within.

Day 34

Joy in Suffering

Consider it pure joy ... whenever you face trials...

(James 1:2 NIV)

Walter's yearly goal was to ride the state fair's helicopter, but his nagging wife Ethel always complained, "Walter, you know that helicopter ride costs 50 dollars and 50 dollars is 50 dollars." The same response came each season until Walter turned 87. Fortunately, the pilot had pity by making them a deal. If they stayed quiet, the ride was free. If but one sound, it was $50. Upon takeoff, the pilot slowly cranked up the ride. No noise. Then he made death-defying tricks and spirals. Still not a peep. When they landed, the pilot applauded Walter for his restraint. "Well," Walter admitted, "I almost said something when Ethel fell out of the helicopter, then I recalled '50 dollars is 50 dollars.'"[65]

---

65 "Walter Took His Wife Ethel to the State Fair Every Year," Reddit Post, R/Jokes, March 14, 2019, https://www.reddit.com/r/Jokes/comments/b0zv24/walter_took_his_wife_ethel_to_the_state_fair/.

Life's journey is full of unexpected twists and turns. King David knew this helicopter ride all too well. From a simple shepherd boy to the famed slayer of Goliath, David witnessed how fast life could change. He understood deep despair and fervent bliss. Just as God lifted David *"out of the depths"* (Psalm 30:1 NIV), He can lift us out of despair. David writes, *"weeping may tarry for the night, but joy comes with the morning"* (Psalm 30:5b ESV). Yes, suffering is guaranteed for a season, no matter how good or bad we are (Matthew 4:45). At the moment a baby enters the world, the infant instantly experiences pain. Isn't it symbolic that life begins with a cry? Because of sin in this world, we *"...will have to suffer. But cheer up! I [Jesus] has defeated the world"* (John 16:33 CEV).

Because Jesus has overcome the world, we may weep to release the grief we are experiencing, yet David affirms that the joy God promises is as sure as the morning that comes after each night. Though darkness will come for a time, we can take comfort that the season will pass and light will return. At times, it may not feel like our pain is temporary. However, remember that Earth has no sorrow that Heaven cannot heal. Our trust that God has great joy in store for us is much like the joy a woman experiences after childbirth (John 16:21). The best is yet to come.

Good news! We do not have to wait until morning to find joy. We can discover joy right amid sorrow. Unlike happiness, which ends at the beginning of sorrow, joy rises from sorrow that can withstand all grief. We can consider it pure joy whenever we face trials (James 1:2) because God will *"transform the Valley of Trouble into a gateway of hope"* (Hosea 2:15 NLT). By finding purpose in our trials, we can rejoice, knowing that as we endure suffering while choosing joy, God will develop a deeper character in us (Romans 5:3–4). We cannot develop endurance without suffering, which is why joy is best sown in broken ground.

When the ground was broken for Jesus' rugged tree to be hung, Christ found joy in enduring the cross since He found joy in us (Hebrews 12:1–2). We, too, can find joy in our suffering because we find joy in Him—the source of joy. We can make it a lifestyle to cry out to God, "It is well with my soul," because what was meant for evil, God intended for good (Genesis 50:20).

> **If a cross can become a blessing, so can the thorn in our flesh.**

Just as Jesus exchanged the meaning of the cross from a symbol of torture to one of hope and salvation, He gives [us] the grace to do the same ... If a cross can become a blessing, so can ... [the thorn in our flesh].[66]

Death-defying twists and turns of a helicopter ride may be a symbol of torture for most, yet a thrill of joy for others. Every joy in this world has a side of suffering, and as resurrection people, every suffering has a side of joy. For those of faith, there is security in knowing that our ticket has been paid for and there is no chance of falling out of God's harness (Romans 8:35). Now that is worth more than any $50 ride. After all, eternal joy is eternal joy.

---

[66] "Quote by Joni Eareckson Tada, February 1, 2009," Daily Christian Quotes, August 9, 2015, https://www.dailychristianquote.com/tag/disability/.

Action Challenge: Rejoice with those who rejoice; mourn with those who mourn (Romans 12:15). By choosing joy now, we can comfort others later who share a dreadful journey (2 Corinthians 1:3–7).

_____

_____

_____

_____

_____

_____

_____

Prayer: O Good Shepherd, take over my cockpit when I fly through the mountains and valleys. Teach me real joy during sorrow. Show me Your presence is all I need. In Jesus' name, amen.

Suffering expands the soul's capacity for joy.

Day 35

Joy in Tears

Those who sow with tears will reap with songs of joy.

(Psalm 126:5 NIV)

Tiny Tim was in the garden filling in a hole when his neighbor Bob gazed over the fence. Curious about what the mischievous boy was up to, Bob politely asked Tim what he was doing. Tears flowed as Tim described how his goldfish had died and how he just buried it. Bob became concerned and then inquired why the hole was awfully big. Tim patted down the last heap of earth, and then he shot back, "That's because he's inside your stupid cat!"[67]

---

[67] Hodgin, 2004, p. 274.

Has our garden become a graveyard for rotten farewells or a grove for ripened fruit? Psalm 126 speaks about how we can reap a harvest with songs of joy by making a lifestyle of sowing the ground with our tears. When the exiled Israelites journeyed to Babylon for seventy years, they sowed many tears that eventually reaped many songs of joy. And so, God ushered them back. The prophet Isaiah predicted this, *"Those the LORD has rescued will return. They will enter Zion with singing; everlasting joy will crown their heads. Gladness and joy will overtake them, and sorrow and sighing will flee away"* (Isaiah 51:11 NIV).

Two images blossom from Psalm 126. The first image is of the Lord miraculously restoring Israel to her home, an undeserved work that is all of Him. The second is that of God providentially working in our efforts while we wait. Translation for today: pray as though it depends on God, work as though it depends on us. Better yet, pray and work as though it all depended on God working through us. The Lord may choose to perform a miracle, or He may choose a slow but certain work of sowing and reaping. Yes, even in times of sorrow, there is work to be done. That good work will bear good fruit of joy in our lives.

Galatians 6:9 (NIV) gives us encouragement: *"Let us not become weary in doing good, for at the proper time we will reap a harvest if we do not give up."* While the present, fallen, sinful age in which we live is a season of tears, mourning, and crying (Revelation 21:4), we must commit to doing good even if it is difficult (1 Peter 4:19).

Crying is a perfectly natural emotion, for it brings tears that are simply words the heart cannot express. Holding back tears only drowns the heart rather than watering our future harvest of joy. Jesus showed us how to weep (John 11:35). He not only shed tears of sorrow but tears of joy, as there is a season to weep, laugh, mourn, and dance (Ecclesiastes 3:1, 4). Few feelings are more intense, comforting, and healing than crying tears of joy. No wonder, on average, we cry more out of happiness than heartbreak.

Like the Israelites who cried tears of joy when God rescued them, we can cry tears of joy when we experience that exciting feeling from a kind word, gesture, embrace, or shared moment. Tears of joy can also occur when we are triumphant after a great deal of time, effort, and sacrifice. Joyful tears come when we are captivated by God's creation, such as sunrise or birth. Tears of joy flow when we cry with laughter with people we love. Why? Because shared joy is double joy; a shared tear is half a tear.

God cares enough to keep a record of all our tears and to one day wipe them away for good (Psalm 56:8; Isiah 25:8)! Tearful joy in God will be replaced with tearless joy in God. In the meantime, we must be buried with Christ, not in contempt of a neighbor's cat. Let not the hole in our hearts be filled with earthly vices nor unshed tears that could have been sown to reap songs of joy.

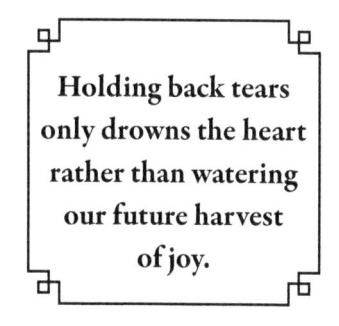

> **Holding back tears only drowns the heart rather than watering our future harvest of joy.**

Action Challenge: Start your mornings with God by crying out to Him to help meet your needs (Psalm 88:13). What has He done to assure your tears will turn to joy? How do you live in the tension between grieving painful times and living in the joy of Christ?

_____

_____

_____

_____

_____

_____

_____

Prayer: Father, hear my cries and count my tears, for they are many. Help me to sow these tears so that a harvest of joy can enrich my life and restore my hope in Christ. In Jesus' name, amen.

A joyful harvest comes by way of sown tears.

Day 36

Joy in Weakness

That is why, for Christ's sake, I delight in weakness...

(2 Corinthians 12:9 NIV)

A lion wandered through the jungle. When he saw a tiger, he roared and beat his chest, saying, "I'm the king of the jungle." The tiger tucked his tail and ran. When the lion saw a gorilla, he roared, "I'm the king of the jungle." Naturally, the gorilla climbed the nearest tree. Then the lion boldly roared at an elephant, "I'm the king of the jungle," at which point the elephant reached out with his trunk, grabbed the lion, spun him around, and slammed him against a tree, where he laid there limp as stars circled his head. At last, the lion staggered to his feet, looked over at the elephant, and said, "Some animals just don't know how to take a joke."[68]

---

[68] Lord, 2017.

"**P**ower over others is weakness disguised as strength."[69] While bullies themselves are inherently weak, we may feel weakened in the process. The Apostle Paul summarizes four such weaknesses he experienced that limited his response but not his resolve: insults, hardships, persecutions, and calamities (2 Corinthians 12:10). In this reference, he did not view weakness as imperfect behaviors or sins like gluttony or lust per se. Instead, he saw how we are all weak because we all have certain wounds or situations beyond our control that make us look weak, things we probably could eliminate if we had the right portion of strength.

Even if we had enough strength to react, it would look different than how the world would use that strength. Jesus directs us not to return evil for evil (Matthew 5:38–42). Paul tells us that *"when we are cursed, we bless; when we are persecuted, we endure it; when we are slandered, we answer kindly"* (1 Corinthians 4:12–13 NIV). Those who equate strength with a hearty comeback will see a Christian's lifestyle of kind responses as weak and frail. Still, there is hope. If Paul could rejoice in his weakness, so too can we be filled with Christ's strength in our weakness and experience great joy, even in situations we do not enjoy.

Notice that Paul did not boast about the thorn that made him weak but the very weakness that made his faith stronger in his Savior. He explains how when he is weak, Christ's sufficient power "rests on" him (2 Corinthians 12:9). In Greek, the compound word for "rests on" means to make a dwelling place or pitch a tent. The phrase carries the idea that Jesus is the glory of God who has set up a tent among us just as the shekinah glory of God dwelt among God's people in the Tabernacle of the Old Testament. Weakness is the tent where Jesus' glory dwells.

Let us journey to the tent where the Lord dwells. When we abide in His tent, His presence will give us both joy and strength (Psalm

---

69 "Quote by Ekhart Tolle," BrainyQuote, 2024, https://www.brainyquote.com/quotes/eckhart_tolle_571619.

16:11), much like it did for Moses the stutter who dwelt, and God gave him strength to speak before Pharaoh… or Esther the insecure queen who dwelt, and God gave her strength to advocate for her people… or Elijah the exhausted prophet who dwelt, and God delivered him from the psychopathic Jezebel. The joy of the Lord became their strength, and it can reside in our hearts as well (Nehemiah 8:10).

Weakness is no joke. When we set up camp in this ruthless world, at times, we will feel debilitated and helpless, as though our tent is utterly surrounded by lions, tigers, and gorillas. And yet, the King of Kings is no bully. He entrusts weakness to us so that we might dwell in His joy and strength (Isaiah 40:29).

> **The King of Kings is no bully. He entrusts weakness to us so that we might dwell in His joy and strength.**

Action Challenge: A problem defined is half-solved, so identify your weakness. Share that weakness with a small group of holy friends who will edify, bring accountability, and let you confess a need for prayer, strength, healing, and joy (James 5:16).

_____

_____

_____

_____

_____

_____

_____

Prayer: Lord, thank You for those things in my life that keep me weak and dependent on You to be my strength. I surrender my fears, anxieties, and limitations to You alone. In Jesus' name, amen.

Joy begins when pride ends so we can accept our weakness.

Day 37

Joy in Poverty

Happy are those who ... are spiritually poor...

(Matthew 5:3 GNT)

A man on vacation was strolling along the sidewalk outside his hotel. Suddenly, he was attracted by the screams of a woman kneeling in front of a child near a ditch. The man knew enough to determine that the child had swallowed a coin. Seizing the child by the heels, the man held him up, turned him upside down, gave him a few shakes, and a quarter dropped to the sidewalk. "Oh, thank you, sir!" cried the woman. "You seemed to know just how to get it out of him. Are you a physician?"

"No, ma'am," he said. "I'm with the Internal Revenue Service." [70]

---

[70] Excavating Contractor, Vol. 53–54, (Excavating Engineer Publishing Company, 1959), p. 56.

Coughing up money does not eternally save us. We can no more buy our way into Heaven than we can work our way into the Kingdom. Jesus teaches us in His first recorded sermon of all time, *"Blessed are the poor in spirit, for theirs is the kingdom of heaven"* (Matthew 5:3 NIV). Why does He begin with this? Because being poor in spirit is the fundamental posture of a Kingdom of Heaven citizen. Every other state of being flows from this one.

Notice the text does not say we must give up all we own to follow God; that was a lesson for the rich young ruler (Matthew 19:22). Jesus exposed the man's true weakness—greed, indulgence, and materialism. The rich young man thought he was rich but walked away from Christ with nothing. "There is nothing wrong with men possessing riches. The wrong comes when riches possess men."[71]

Jesus does not instruct Christians to make a lifestyle of living poor––to be free of material belongings or money. Instead, He desires a lifestyle of living *"poor in spirit."* Scripture does not say "money is the root of all evil," but the *"love of money is"* (1 Timothy 6:10 NIV). Money is not the issue. The heart is. A helpful way to understand what Jesus meant is to put the word "humble" in place of the word "poor." When we come to God, we must recognize our sin, our spiritual barrenness and poverty. We cannot be filled until we are first empty. When we are full of ourselves, we cannot be hungry for God. A person who is not willing to turn from his self-sufficiency, possessions, false religion, or selfishness will miss out on the grace, blessing, and joy in Christ (James 4:6). If selfishness is the key to being doleful, then self*less*ness must be the key to being joyful.

> We cannot be filled until we are first empty. When we are full of ourselves, we can't be hungry for God.

---

[71] Quoatable, "Quote by Billy Graham," Quoatable, February 3, 2023, https://www.quoatable.com/billy-graham-quote-there-is-nothing-wrong-with-men-possessing-riches-the-wrong-comes-when-riches-possess-men/.

Believers who are "spiritually poor" will be "happy" or "blessed." The Greek term Jesus uses here is *makarios*, yet the closest English version is diluted as "happy" or "blessed" even though *makarios* literally means "whoopie, full of blissful joy and excitement!"[72] The joy of the Spirit overflows when poor in spirit.

By walking in the center of the sidewalk, we avoid the pious rich-in-spirit ditch (Romans 12:3), or the having-wealth-is-unspiritual ditch because we live minimally. Walking alert, we acknowledge our spiritual poverty before God since we have been turned upside down and shaken empty of any spiritual "richness" that might be applied to our credit. He paid a debt He did not owe; we owed a debt we could not pay… tax free. As the Great Physician, God can cure us of our spiritual bankruptcy because forgiveness was bought with the precious blood of Jesus Christ.

---

[72] "Makarios – The Key to Happiness (Word of the Week) – Ezra Project," Ezra, 2023, https://ezraproject.com/2018-10-1-makarios-the-key-to-happiness-word-of-the-week/.

Action Challenge: Devote your currency of time to making a lifestyle of rising each morning at daybreak this week (Mark 1:35). Invite God to audit the spiritual poverty of your soul. Cough up what weighs you down so that you might be light-footed to do His will and run with joy.

___

___

___

___

___

___

___

___

Prayer: Search me, O Lord, break the bank of my heart for what breaks Yours. Turn me upside down, shake me empty of earthly treasures that make me stumble so I can radiate the fullness of joy and that others may taste a slice of heaven. In Jesus' name, amen.

We must first bankrupt our hearts before striking it rich in Kingdom joy.

Day 38

Joy in Discipline

All discipline for the moment seems not to be joyful, but ... yields the peaceful fruit of righteousness.

(Hebrews 12:11 NASB)

Little Bobby struggled in math, even after personal tutors, mentors, and flash cards. So, his parents tried enrolling him in a Catholic school. Day after day, Bobby would come home and go straight to his room, disciplining himself routinely to study math. Before long, little Bobby brought home his report card. Momma was shocked, yet joyful to see an "A" in math. Unable to contain herself, she asked Bobby what was the difference maker...the books, the structure, the uniforms, the nuns? He sheepishly quipped, "Well, on the first day of school, when I saw that guy nailed to the plus sign, I knew they weren't fooling around."[73]

---

[73] "Jokes of the Day for Friday, 10 September 2010: Catholic School," JOKES OF THE DAY, 2010, https://jokesoftheday.net/jokes-archive/2010/09/10/.

Whatever our motivation, we should discipline our lives, so God will not have to. The journey in studying math takes discipline, as does the journey in daily routines like making our bed, eating fewer calories, or exercising consistently. The more we practice these basic routines, the more our habits will spill over into other disciplines, such as the spiritual disciplines of Bible study, prayer, fasting, and meditation. If there were a road construction sign posted along our pathway, it would read, "The inconvenience is temporary, but the improvement is permanent."

God brings about a permanent transformation of our lives through a lifestyle of growth by way of spiritual disciplines. We will not know real joy until there is a transforming work within us. Many people try to speed their way to joy by finding temporary satisfaction in the things of this world when, in reality, nothing constructive has happened in their lives. God has not become their routine refueling station, and so their happiness is fleeting. Legalists might go to the other extreme by practicing spiritual disciplines to become self-righteous like the Pharisees, yet Paul emphatically states the goal of discipline and taking control of our habits is *"for the purpose of godliness"* (1 Timothy 4:7 NASB).

Motivation for pleasing God is what gets us started. Habit is what keeps us going. At first glance, the word "discipline" does not sound very motivational or joyful on its own, especially since "we must all suffer one of two things: the pain of discipline or the pain of disappointment."[74] And yet, with the right motivation, spiritual discipline becomes the means

> **Motivation for pleasing God is what gets us started. Habit is what keeps us going.**

---

[74] "Quote by Jin Rohn," Gary Fox, June 20, 2017, https://www.garyfox.co/quotes/must-suffer-one-two-things-pain-discipline-pain-regret-disappointment/.

to godliness and godliness the means to joy (Hebrews 12:11). Even secular research reveals that self-disciplined people are happier.

We must be careful, however, not to take our eyes off the road because no joy can be found swerving onto unpaved areas only because we stopped regularly practicing habits that join us with God. Solomon wisely summarizes, *"He dies for lack of discipline, and because of his great folly he is led astray"* (Proverbs 5:23 ESV).

Each of us has a choice to either succumb to our own devices and be led astray or submit to God's disciplines and be rewarded with a satisfying report card. The Lord is not fooling around when He says that He wants us to know Him. We must do whatever it takes... personal tutors, mentors, or even flashcards... to help us better understand that His Son is more than just some guy nailed to a plus sign. He is the author of both addition and subtraction. It is He who can exponentially multiply the joy in our lives if we simply practice the spiritual disciplines with a pure heart and a "right spirit" (Psalm 51:10–12).

Action Challenge: If practicing spiritual disciplines feels like drudgery, try a new approach.

> *Rather than studying Scripture by yourself, do it in groups. Instead of reading long passages of the Bible, create artwork while meditating on single verses. Instead of making long lists of prayer requests, sit in silence and ask God to fill [your] mind.*[75]

Concentrate on enjoying God.

_____

_____

_____

_____

_____

_____

Prayer: Oh God, guard the minutes and hours You have given me. Bolster my self-discipline so that I can become more like You and receive an outpouring of divine joy. In Jesus' name, amen.

Joy is a journey; discipline is the vehicle.

---

[75] Heather Caliri, "How to Practice Spiritual Disciplines from a Heart of Joy, Not Guilt," iBelieve.com, 2018, https://www.ibelieve.com/faith/how-to-practice-spiritual-disciplines-from-a-heart-of-joy-not-guilt.html.

Day 39

Joy in Persecution

"Rejoice in that day [of persecution] and leap for joy, because great is your reward in heaven."

(Luke 6:23a NIV)

A Sunday School teacher handed out rewards for those who answered her questions correctly. She asked the question if she had sold her house and all her belongings, would she get to Heaven? "No!" all the children answered. The teacher went on to ask if she was flying in a plane with turbulence as it was falling out of the sky, yet she gave her only parachute to another passenger without one. Would she get into Heaven? Again, the answer was, "No!" Ms. Roxy finally concluded by asking the central question of how then would she get into Heaven? A five-year-old boy shouted from the back, "You gotta be dead!"[76]

---

[76] Joc Anderson Psyd, The Author of Love: Understanding a Misunderstood God, (Bloomington: WestBow Press, 2011), p. 91.

The surest ticket to Heaven is by dying on behalf of the Lord (Matthew 24:13). And yet, not all persecution leads to death. Jesus' statement that anyone who endures to the end does not mean our salvation is dependent on our ability to remain saved; instead, it is a promise of perseverance. Those who have a lifestyle of grace to persist to the end are those who are authentically saved by grace. Persecution will reveal our true colors. Jesus says, *"Because of the increase of wickedness, the love of most will grow cold"* (Matthew 24:12 NIV). The ones who fall away from Christ were never saved to begin with. However, those who endure incitements and stand firm in their journey of faith demonstrate they are children of God (1 Peter 1:5).

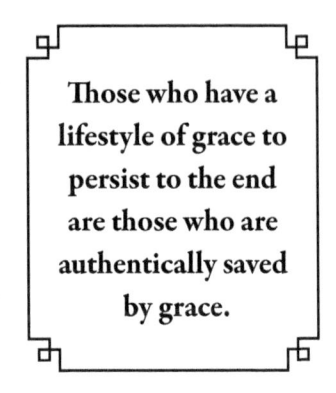

> Those who have a lifestyle of grace to persist to the end are those who are authentically saved by grace.

Perhaps the secret ingredient to enduring persecution is joy. Jesus declares that when we are being persecuted, we must leap for joy because our reward is not here on this earth but in Heaven (Luke 6:23). Look at some biblical examples. When the apostles were shamed for Jesus' sake, they miraculously *"left the presence of the council, rejoicing that they were counted worthy to suffer dishonor for the name"* (Acts 5:41 ESV).

The writer of Hebrews praises the Jewish Christians who miraculously bore a degree of physical abuse with joy, knowing what awaited them in Heaven was far more valuable (Hebrews 10:32). Paul celebrated the churches of Macedonia because, despite their great trial of affliction and persecution, they miraculously experienced overflowing joy (2 Corinthians 8:1-2). If the early Christians could endure hardship in the past, we can withstand it today. But how?

It is easier for a camel to go through the eye of a needle than for us to feel joy when reviled, persecuted, and slandered. Jesus commands us to rejoice and be glad and to control our feelings when that goes against all-natural human ability. When we are reviled, lied about, and abused as Jesus' followers, how can we emit joy and gladness when our impulse is to retaliate (Matthew 5:11–12)? We cannot. *"Humanly speaking, it is impossible. But not with God. Everything is possible with God"* (Mark 10:27 NLT). He gives us a miracle of grace and joy when we suffer for Him.

    The question is not a matter of *if* but *when* persecution will come (2 Timothy 3:12). Obeying Christ brings opposition. Trying to avert it is like trying to pilot a plane without turbulence; it comes with the territory. If we are persecuted because we cherish His values or declare He is the only way, Jesus says, "Rejoice!" Cheers, we have hit turbulence, and we are flying in the Kingdom. Though our path will not be free from barriers, we are in the same airways as the apostles and heroes of the faith who preceded us. Moreover, our reward is greater than an airline pin with wings. The reward is inconceivable, preserved for us in Heaven.

Action Challenge: Prepare yourself for when persecution comes. Do not be surprised by it but fully expect it to happen (Matthew 24:9). Avoid feeling ashamed because persecution is a tremendous gift from God (Philippians 1:29). Fix our gaze heavenward; this is not our home; we are just passing through (2 Corinthians 4:17–18).

_____
_____
_____
_____
_____
_____
_____

Prayer: Loving Father, when I am being persecuted, saturate me with Your miracle of grace. Replace my fear with joy when I face hostility resulting from my holy living. In Jesus' name, amen.

Persecution gives us living joy and dying rest.

Day 40

Joy in Perpetuity

Always be joyful.

(1 Thessalonians 5:16 NLT)

A lady was going on her very first bus trip across the state. She was quite nervous but also more than a little irritating to Sam, the driver, and other passengers with her endless comments, nagging, and questions. After several hours of non-stop talk right behind the driver's ear, she asked Sam, "How do you know where my stop is and how will I know where my stop is and is there a billboard and when will I know it's time to get off the bus and…"

Sam interrupted her as he looked in the mirror above his head, "Lady, you'll know it when you see the big smile on my face!"[77]

---

[77] "[Lady Nervous on a Bus]," Author Unknown, n.d.

If non-stop "nagging is the repetition of unpalatable truths,"[78] then, what follows it is that the truth hurts. When it comes to biblical truth, we are not immunized from hurt or pain. In fact, we are to "always be full of joy" (Philippians 4:4 NLT). Being always full of joy does not mean that we will never feel depressed or sad. When we consider all of Scripture, we see that the shortest Greek New Testament verse reads, "Rejoice always" (1 Thessalonians 5:16 NIV). Meanwhile, the shortest verse in the English New Testament is "Jesus wept" (John 11:35 NIV). Do not treat these statements as contradictory; instead, recall how Jesus could weep while having fullness of joy during the crucifixion (John 15:11).

For the Christian, rejoicing is to take place at all times. We rejoice always in spite of our life, not in place of it. Joy can co-exist with awful sadness, as exemplified when Paul was persecuted, shipwrecked, and stoned. Rather than complain, he focused on rejoicing. Even in the midst of physical and emotional pain, we can be like the apostle and rejoice. But how? We rejoice not in our circumstances but *"in the Lord"* (Philippians 4:4 NIV).

Surely, in this fallen world, we will endure many circumstances that will not make us happy. The joy of believers is not based on agreeable circumstances. Rather, it is based on our relationship with God. Christians will face trouble in this world, but we can rejoice *in* the Lord and delight *in* Him, knowing that these trials will improve our character (James 1:2–4). By abiding *in* Him, His supernatural joy in us is what makes our joy perpetual. He gives His people ongoing joy when we walk in obedience to His Word, including the command

> **The only way to be happy in Jesus is to be dreadfully unhappy without Him.**

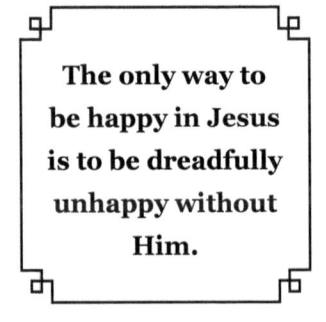

78 "Quote by Edith Summerskill, Baroness Summerskill: Speech to Married Women's Association, House of Commons, 14 July 1960, in The Times 15 July 1960," A-Z Quotes, 2024, https://www.azquotes.com/quote/583237.

to *"rejoice always."* Paul repeats this directive for emphasis as if to say, "rejoicing always is possible."

When we choose to rejoice always in the Lord, we acknowledge what God has done for us through the life, death, burial, and resurrection of the Lord Jesus Christ. Should not that alone bring us exceeding joy? In Philippians 3:1, many who claimed to be Christian were not relying only upon Christ's shed blood for salvation but rather in themselves alone (Philippians 3:2, 4–6). The only way to be happy in Jesus is to be dreadfully unhappy without Him. Choosing joy is a matter of obedience, not temperament.

Truth be told, it is time for truth in a truthless time: a holy lifestyle keeps our joy continually overflowing despite the irritation others may bring along the journey. Satan will try to interrupt our perpetual state of joy with vexing passengers. And yet, we must resist the temptation to lose our cool and joy, as this will portray an unattractive billboard for our Lord. No matter the circumstance, let us exemplify joy with a big smile on our faces.

Action Challenge: There is no coincidence that the Bible's most frequent command is to "sing," and its longest book is a hymn book. When you are feeling down, read the Psalms and create your tunes to the words. Obeying this simple command of singing praises to the Lord will rekindle your joy.

_____

_____

_____

_____

_____

_____

Prayer: Precious Lord, I have many reasons to rejoice always, for You are worthy of all my praise. Thank you for making me, saving me, and never leaving me. May I never cease to rejoice in You all the days of my life. In Jesus' name, amen.

Unceasing joy depends not on changing winds but winds of the One who never changes.

Epilogue

CULTIVATING A LIFETIME OF JOY

As you conclude your forty-day journey through *Journey in Joy*, may the echoes of lessons learned and spiritual truths embraced resonate in the depths of your soul. The imagery of that hot summer day, desperately searching for a gas station to refuel, serves as a metaphor for the constant need to nourish your spiritual journey. Much like a vehicle requiring fuel for optimal performance, your soul craves regular fill-ups and tune-ups to keep moving on the road of life.

Just as the devotional plan emphasizes, waiting until your spiritual tank is empty is quite risky. The call is to be proactive in maintaining your spiritual vitality, choosing the premium grade of divine truths and principles over the diluted fuel of worldly distractions. One of those key truths comes from Nehemiah 8:10 (ESV), which reminds us that "the joy of the LORD is our strength." What is represented here is an unshakeable joy that completes us, a joy found in abiding in His presence. This joy becomes a Fruit of the Spirit, a gift from God that requires our willingness to abide in Him. The metaphor of growing tomatoes emphasizes the need for regular attention, nourishment, and adherence to God's plan for spiritual growth.

The epiphany here is clear: just as a gardener cannot will a ripe tomato into existence, you cannot manufacture true joy on your own. Joy, as a Fruit of the Spirit, is a gift from God, cultivated through a relationship with Him. Joy becomes the natural outgrowth of abiding in Him, allowing His Spirit to work within you.

In the biblical examples, believers and unbelievers experience a form of joy—common grace. However, the joy offered through a relationship with God is deeper, enduring, and transcends the fleeting happiness based on external circumstances. As you navigate your spiritual journey, it is crucial to distinguish between the superficial joy of the world and the profound, abiding joy found in the Lord.

The joy described in your forty-day journey is spiritual joy, hidden within the heart like an underground wellspring. It is a joy that remains in the face of suffering, rooted in the Word of God. It is not dependent on situational happenings; rather, it is a joy that can thrive even in the midst of adversity.

Completing the forty-day devotional is not the end; it is the beginning of a whole new lifestyle of living. Satan may attempt to steal your joy, and challenges may knock on your door, but this is precisely when the joy of the Lord should blossom in your soul. Resist the allure of worldly pleasures, remain rooted in God's truth, and choose joy even before the pain begins.

Index

Bible Translations

Bible	Abbreviation
Contemporary English Version	CEV
English Standard Version	ESV
Easy-to-Read Version	ERV
Good News Translation	GNT
Holman Christian Standard Bible	HCSB
King James Version	KJV
The Message	MSG
Montgomery New Testament	MNT
New American Standard	NASB
New English Translation	NET
New International Version	NIV
New King James Version	NKJV
New Living Translation	NLT
New Revised Standard Version	NRSV
Revised Standard Version	RSV

References

"60 Thanksgiving Jokes to Tell Around the Reunion Table." 2022. *Little Day Out* (blog). January 19, 2022. https://www.littledayout.com/thanksgiving-jokes-to-tell-around-the-reunion-table/.

"131+ Listen Jokes and Funny Puns." n.d. JokoJokes. Accessed January 28, 2024. https://jokojokes.com/listen-jokes.html.

"A Guy Looking for Work." 2007. Jokes by Scout Life. May 27, 2007. https://jokes.scoutlife.org/jokes/a-guy-looking-for-work/.

"A Man Goes on Vacation to Israel with His Wife and His Stepmother." 2018. Reddit Post. *R/Jokes*. https://www.reddit.com/r/Jokes/comments/982rbu/a_man_goes_on_vacation_to_israel_with_his_wife/.

Anderson Psyd, Joc. 2011. *The Author of Love: Understanding a Misunderstood God*. Bloomington: WestBow Press.

"A Quote by Charles Haddon Spurgeon." 2024. Goodreads, Inc. 2024. https://www.goodreads.com/quotes/397346-a-bible-that-s-falling-apart-usually-belongs-to-someone-who.

"A Quote by Ricky Gervais." 2024. Goodreads, Inc. 2024. https://www.goodreads.com/quotes/9260914-if-you-try-to-please-everyone-you-ll-please-no-one.

"A Quote by Roger A. Caras." 2024. Goodreads. 2024. https://www.goodreads.com/quotes/19168-dogs-are-not-our-whole-life-but-they-make-our.

Assey, Gerard. 2020. *Christian Jokes for the 'Serious Religious' Folks!: A Preachers & Christian Ministers' Companion*. Independently published.

"'Attitude' Adjustment." 2021. Hot Springs Sentinel Record. September 19, 2021. https://www.hotsr.com/news/2021/sep/19/attitude-adjustment/.

Author Unknown. n.d.-a. "[Anecdote: Boy Asks Dad How It Feels to Have a Perfect Son.]"

———. n.d.-b. "[Joke: Mistaken Flying Instructor]."

———. n.d.-c. "[Lady Nervous on a Bus]."

Blackman, Lucy. 2011. *Have You Heard the One About . . . Religion.* Bloomington: iUniverse Publishing.

Bonhoeffer, Dietrich, and Eric Metaxas. 1995. *The Cost of Discipleship.* First Edition. New York: Touchstone.

Burkhart, Austin. 2015. "Avodah: A Seamless Life of Work, Worship, and Service." Institute for Faith, Work & Economics. March 31, 2015. https://tifwe.org/avodah-a-life-of-work-worship-and-service/.

Caliri, Heather. 2018. "How to Practice Spiritual Disciplines from a Heart of Joy, Not Guilt." iBelieve.com. 2018. https://www.ibelieve.com/faith/how-to-practice-spiritual-disciplines-from-a-heart-of-joy-not-guilt.html.

"Contentment." 2024. Etymology of Contentment by Etymonline. 2024. https://www.etymonline.com/word/contentment.

"Didn't See That Coming." n.d. The Cybersalt Site. Accessed January 29, 2024. https://www.cybersalt.org/clean-jokes/didnt-see-that-coming.

"Dilemian: Two Hunters and a Bear Story, Author Unknown." n.d. Sermon Illustrations. Accessed January 16, 2024. https://www.sermonillustrations.com/a-z/d/dilemma.htm.

Evans, Tony. 2009. *Tony Evans' Book of Illustrations: Stories, Quotes, and Anecdotes from More Than 30 Years of Preaching and Public Speaking.* New edition. Chicago, IL: Moody Publishers.

"Everest Jokes - 77 Hilarious Everest Jokes." n.d. Upjoke.com. Accessed January 29, 2024. https://upjoke.com/everest-jokes.

Excavating Contractor. 1959. Vol. 53–54. Excavating Engineer Publishing Company.

Ferguson, Barry. 2016. In *Collision Course: How to Harness the Power of Love to Heal Your Broken Life*, 178. New York: Morgan Publishing.

Gambles, Sarah. 2023. "Do You Put up Christmas Decorations before or after Thanksgiving?" Yahoo News. November 26, 2023. https://news.yahoo.com/put-christmas-decorations-thanksgiving-052017418.html.

Gleghorn, Michael. n.d. "Quote by C. S. Lewis in: Astrology: Do the Heavens Declare the Destiny of Man?" https://michaelgleghorn.com/artAstrology.php.

"Great Spoil Sermon by Charles Haddon Spurgeon | January 22, 1882." 2017. The Spurgeon Library: The Spurgeon Center and Midwestern Baptist Theological Seminary. 2017. https://www.spurgeon.org/resource-library/sermons/great-spoil/.

"Her Husband Typed His Wife's Email Wrong. The Result? So Bad It's Funny!!!" 2014. Littlethings. 2014. https://littlethings.com/lifestyle/wrong-email/293635-1.

Hodgin, Michael. 1998. *1001 More Humorous Illustrations for Public Speaking: Fresh, Timely, and Compelling Illustrations for Preachers, Teachers, and Speakers.* Grand Rapids, MI: Zondervan.

———. 2004. *1002 Humorous Illustrations for Public Speaking: Fresh, Timely, Compelling Illustrations for Preachers, Teachers, and Speakers.* Illustrated edition. Grand Rapids, MI: Zondervan.

Hollingsworth, Mary. 2011. *The One Year Devotional of Joy and Laughter: 365 Inspirational Meditations to Brighten Your Day.* Carol Stream, IL: Tyndale House Publishers.

Hopman, Gerry. 2005. *Kids Say the "Doggonest" Things.* USA: G. H. Hopman and Associates Ltd.

"Humor." n.d. Ofthisandthat. Accessed January 29, 2024. https://ofthisandthat.org/Humor.html.

Janowski, Dano. 2020. *Rabbit and Cat's Pandemic Jokes #7 For Such a Time as This: Even in Pandemics You Gotta Laugh.* (Rabbit & Cat Comics, May 3, 2020).

"Joke: After God Created Adam, Author Unknown." 2020. Reddit Post. *R/Jokes*. www.reddit.com/r/Jokes/comments/ie86sy/after_god_created_adam_adam_came_to_god_and_said/.

"Joke: Blind Date – JokeBarn.com." 1999. *JokeBarn.com* (blog). August 25, 1999. https://www.jokebarn.com/388/blind-date/.

"Joke: Do Not Enter, Author Unknown." n.d. Humor | Ministry127. Accessed January 28, 2024. https://ministry127.com/resources/illustrations/humor?page=2.

"Joke: One Day a Man Went to an Auction, Author Unknown." 2018. Reddit Post. *R/Jokes*. https://www.reddit.com/r/Jokes/comments/85s6yg/one_day_a_man_went_to_an_auction_while_there_he/.

"Jokes of the Day for Friday, 10 September 2010: Catholic School." 2010. JOKES OF THE DAY. 2010. https://jokesoftheday.net/jokes-archive/2010/09/10/.

Lauterbach, Rondi. 2021. "Faithfulness: A Promise That Leads to Joy." *Rondi Lauterbach* (blog). March 16, 2021. https://www.rondilauterbach.com/2021/03/16/faithfulness-a-promise-that-leads-to-joy/.

"Let Everything That Has Breathe Praise the Lord! | Sermon Joke by Dr. Madana Kumar." n.d. Faith Lutheran Church. Accessed January 29, 2024. https://www.faithlutheranchurch.org/sermons/let-everything-has-breath-praise-lord.

"Little Faith and Great Faith Sermon by Charles Haddon Spurgeon, November 2, 1890." 2017. The Spurgeon Library: The Spurgeon Center and Midwestern Baptist Theological Seminary. 2017. https://www.spurgeon.org/resource-library/sermons/little-faith-and-great-faith/.

Lord, Jack. 2017. *Now That's Funny: Humorous Illustrations to Soup Up Your Talks, Sermons, or Speeches*. Eugene, OR: Resource Publications.

"Makarios – The Key to Happiness (Word of the Week) – Ezra Project." 2023. Ezra. 2023. https://ezraproject.com/2018-10-1-makarios-the-key-to-happiness-word-of-the-week/.

"Meaning of Life Jokes - 29 Hilarious Meaning of Life Jokes." n.d. Upjoke.com. Accessed January 28, 2024. https://upjoke.com/meaning-of-life-jokes.

Miller, Paul M., Compiler. 2013. *The World's Greatest Collection of Church Jokes: Nearly 500 Hilarious, Good-Natured Jokes and Stories.* Uhrichsville, OH: Barbour Publishing.

"My Hope Is Built on Nothing Less by Edward Mote, 1834." n.d. Hymnary.org. Accessed January 15, 2024. https://hymnary.org/text/my_hope_is_built_on_nothing_less.

"Nghiep Gia Hoang, St. Anthony Church, Weiner." 2023. Catholic Diocese of Little Rock. 2023. https://www.dolr.org/clergy/nghiep-gia-hoang.

Palmer, J. 2020. "Joy By the Answer of the Mouth." *Living Water Ministries* (blog). October 22, 2020. https://livingwaterministries.blog/2020/10/22/joy-by-the-answer-of-the-mouth/.

Phillips, Bob. 1990. *The All-New Clean Joke Book.* Eugene, OR: Harvest House Publishers.

Piper, John. 2004. *When I Don't Desire God Publisher: Crossway Books.* Wheaton, Illinois: Crossway.

"Prayers for Joy in God's Creation: Prayers from the Common Book of Prayer." 2024. Washington Free Methodist Church. 2024. https://pluto.sitetackle.com/16409/?subpages/Common%20Prayer.shtml.

Quoatable. 2023. "Quote by Billy Graham." Quoatable. February 3, 2023. https://www.quoatable.com/billy-graham-quote-there-is-nothing-wrong-with-men-possessing-riches-the-wrong-comes-when-riches-possess-men/.

"Quote by Charles Shultz." 2021. *My Geek Wisdom* (blog). September 4, 2021. https://mygeekwisdom.com/2021/09/04/i-love-mankind-its-people-i-cant-stand/.

"Quote by Edith Summerskill, Baroness Summerskill: Speech to Married Women's Association, House of Commons, 14 July 1960, in The

Times 15 July 1960." 2024. A-Z Quotes. 2024. https://www.azquotes.com/quote/583237.

"Quote by Ekhart Tolle." 2024. BrainyQuote. 2024. https://www.brainyquote.com/quotes/eckhart_tolle_571619.

"Quote by Elder Dallin H. Oaks." 2024. A-Z Quotes. 2024. https://www.azquotes.com/quote/864259.

"Quote by Fern Bernstein: Mah Jongg Mondays: A Memoir about Friendship, Love, and Faith." n.d. Goodreads, Inc. Accessed January 29, 2024. https://www.goodreads.com/quotes/10353137-only-god-can-turn-a-mess-into-a-message-a.

"Quote by Jerome K. Jerome." 2024. Goodreads, Inc. 2024. https://www.goodreads.com/quotes/1407-i-like-work-it-fascinates-me-i-can-sit-and.

"Quote by Jin Rohn." 2017. Gary Fox. June 20, 2017. https://www.garyfox.co/quotes/must-suffer-one-two-things-pain-discipline-pain-regret-disappointment/.

"Quote by John Spence." 2024. Quotefancy. 2024. https://quotefancy.com/quote/1698001/John-Spence-Being-alone-does-not-mean-you-are-lonely-and-being-lonely-does-not-mean-you.

"Quote by Joni Eareckson Tada, February 1, 2009." 2015. Daily Christian Quotes. August 9, 2015. https://www.dailychristianquote.com/tag/disability/.

"Quote by K. B. Meyer." 2011. Famous Quotes & Authors. 2011. https://www.famousquotesandauthors.com/authors/kb__meyer_quotes.html.

"Quote by Matthew Henry." 2024. Grace Quotes. 2024. https://gracequotes.org/author-quote/matthew-henry/.

"Quote by S. Parkes Cadman." 2024. Quotefancy. 2024. https://quotefancy.com/quote/1626882/S-Parkes-Cadman-Nobody-dreams-of-music-in-hell-and-nobody-conceives-of-heaven-without-it.

"Quote by Tony Evans." 2024. Quotefancy. 2024. https://quotefancy.

com/quote/1724205/Tony-Evans-Sometimes-God-lets-you-hit-rock-bottom-so-that-you-will-discover-He-is-the.

Shannon, Robert, and Michael Shannon. 1985. *Celebrating the Birth of Christ*. Cincinnati, Ohio: Standard Publishing.

"The Christian Barber." 2019. ChristiansUnite.com. 2019. https://jokes.christiansunite.com/Bible/The_Christian_Barber.shtml.

Tim, Pastor. 2023. "Expensive Cosmetics." The Cybersalt Site. January 11, 2023. https://www.cybersalt.org/pearly-gates-jokes/expensive-cosmetics.

———. n.d. "Puppy Love." The Cybersalt Site. Accessed January 28, 2024. https://www.cybersalt.org/clean-jokes/puppy-love.

"Travel at 60 Daily Joke: A Husband and Wife Are Flying to Australia." 2019. Starts at 60. January 27, 2019. https://startsat60.com/media/travel/husband-wife-joke-flying-australia-crash-landing.

"Unable to Attend the Funeral." 2020. Reddit Post. *R/Jokes*. https://www.reddit.com/r/Jokes/comments/igxjv7/unable_to_attend_the_funeral_after_his_uncle/.

Unthank, Stephen. 2018. "Music in Worship: Sing with Joy." 2018. https://www.placefortruth.org/blog/music-worship-sing-joy.

"Walter Took His Wife Ethel to the State Fair Every Year." 2019. Reddit Post. *R/Jokes*. https://www.reddit.com/r/Jokes/comments/b0zv24/walter_took_his_wife_ethel_to_the_state_fair/.

Warren, Rick. 2002. *The Purpose Driven Life*. First. Zondervan.

Zuverink, Laurie. 2018. "Joy in Worship." Today Daily Devotional: Reframe Ministries. Today Daily Devotional. Https://todaydevotional.com/. 2018. https://todaydevotional.com/devotions/joy-in-worship.

About the Author

Meet Dr. Daniel W. Thompson, a retired Lieutenant Colonel Chaplain whose remarkable, three-decade military journey spans the Marines, Navy, and Air Force Notably, he served as the senior religious advisor for NATO in Kabul, Afghanistan, marking a zenith in his decorated career. Currently an Adjunct Professor at Regent University and Liberty University, his scholarly prowess extends to an array of contributions in the *Global Encyclopedia*. Rev. Thompson, a board-certified chaplain and pastoral counselor, specializes in marriage care and grief management at *A Quiet Place Counseling*. A passionate educator, he imparts World and American History to high school students at Veritas Academy. Beyond his professional pursuits, this Eagle Scout revels in outdoor pursuits like hiking, camping, and tennis. Dr. Thompson's legacy is one of leadership, mentorship, and an enduring impact on academia, counseling, military service, and community.

Printed in the USA
CPSIA information can be obtained
at www.ICGtesting.com
LVHW021922020424
776193LV00003B/3